MW01056409

GO BY BOAT

Stories of a Maine Island Doctor

CHUCK RADIS

Down East Books

Camden, Maine

𝒟𝓸𝔀𝓷 𝓔𝓪𝓼𝓽 𝓑𝓸𝓸𝓴𝓼

Published by Down East Books
An imprint of The Rowman & Littlefield Publishing Group, Inc.
4501 Forbes Boulevard, Suite 200, Lanham, Maryland 20706
www.rowman.com

Distributed by NATIONAL BOOK NETWORK

Copyright © 2021 by Dr. Chuck Radis

All rights reserved. No part of this book may be reproduced in any form or by any electronic or mechanical means, including information storage and retrieval systems, without written permission from the publisher, except by a reviewer who may quote passages in a review.

British Library Cataloguing in Publication Information Available

Library of Congress Cataloging-in-Publication Data Available

ISBN: 978-1-60893-755-4 (hardcover)
ISBN: 978-1-60893-756-1 (e-book)

∞™ The paper used in this publication meets the minimum requirements of American National Standard for Information Sciences—Permanence of Paper for Printed Library Materials, ANSI/NISO Z39.48-1992.

Acknowledgments

It is not easy practicing medicine or living on a Maine island, nor should it be. To my patients and my patient wife, Sandra, thank you for sticking with me over the long haul. To Jim McCarthy and Betsy Gattis, your encouragement and gentle critiques laid bare how much reworking this story needed when I thought I had crossed the finished line.

AUTHOR'S NOTE

Yohanna Von Tiling, the Queen of Casco Bay, and Captain Bud Perry of Peaks Island are presented as is, their medical histories well known to many in the bay. If you knew them, you understand. The remainder of my characters are blended; the details of their medical histories, and physical descriptions altered to protect their privacy.

CHAPTER ONE

Not every doctor works for every patient.
—Ron Anderson, MD

"Lance it." Bud Perry reached up with the tip of his index finger and felt the swollen edge of the infection beneath his left eye. "Take a blade. Slice it open."

"It's not ready. The infection hasn't come to a head. There's nothing to drain," I answered.

"Lance it. You know it needs to be lanced."

I sucked in my cheeks. "It's. Not. Ready. You have a fever. This is a serious infection. We need to get it under control with intravenous antibiotics in the hospital."

"Forget about the hospital. Give me some pills, and I'll come back tomorrow. I probably nicked the edge of it trimming my beard."

I raised an eyebrow. Mr. Perry's unkempt, gray, tobacco-stained beard billowed out from his chest and flowed across his face like a virgin forest. Through the partially open door, I caught the eye of Kathryn, seated at the front desk. Petite, with olive skin and dark, wavy hair, Kathryn comprises 100 percent of the support staff for the Peaks Island Health Center. She schedules and rooms our patients, records their blood pressure and weight, draws their blood, calls in prescriptions, and has seen Bud Perry bully his way through three previous doctors at the health center.

Several months into my island practice I am mortally close to being the fourth.

"Don't you think it's time you switched to an electric razor?" I suggested, buying time. "If it reaches your blood stream, an infection like

1

this can attach to your artificial heart valve." No reaction. "At least let me draw some blood cultures."

Mr. Perry grunted and offered up an arm as I applied a tourniquet. While a second red-top tube filled, my gaze shifted to an ear sticking out beneath his captain's cap. Leaning inward for a closer look, I examined the top of the ear. The lesion was definitely cancerous—either a squamous cell or basal cell carcinoma.

"I've had that gizmo, whatever it is, on my ear for years. Never mind about that; just give me something for this damn infection on my cheek."

"Mister Perry," I took a deep breath. "You're already blind in one eye; let's make sure we do everything we can to protect the other eye. We can have you in town in no time, start IV antibiotics, and have you home—"

Abruptly, Bud Perry leaned on the handle of his makeshift cane, a cut-off coal shovel, and, pushing himself to his feet, started for the door. "Fine. Maybe Tommy Elkhorn has some pills left over from his prostate infection."

Kathryn knocked on the door. "Can you take a phone call? Cliff Island. They need a house call."

"In a second! Hold on, hold on, Mister Perry," I exhaled in defeat. From the cabinet I counted out sixteen cephalexin and sealed them in an envelope. I am making a deal. It is the best I can get, for now. For all I know, Tommy Elkhorn's pills were prescribed to deworm his cat. "Take two pills, four times a day, with food. Alcohol is not food. The rest of your prescription should be down on the afternoon ferry. I want to see you tomorrow, bright and early. If the blood cultures grow out bacteria, I'm admitting you."

I pulled my pocket calendar from my shirt pocket and wrote, *Call Bud Perry 766-3439 if alive tomorrow and skips appt.*

Emptying the envelope in his palm, Bud looked at the pills skeptically. Suddenly, he was in no particular hurry to leave. He held a pill up to the light and squinted through his sighted eye like an indecisive Cyclops. "You're not giving me sulfa, are you?"

"No, Mister Perry, I'm not giving you sulfa." I involuntarily ground my teeth. Hold on. The man needs help. Try to understand where he's coming from. I placed my hand on his shoulder. "I've checked your chart, and you took this same antibiotic last year and—"

"You know I'm allergic to sulfa," he interrupted. "Laid me out good as dead. But I'll take these pills. What do I know anyway? They're probably better than Tommy's pills." Then he jabbed the end of the coal shovel toward my midsection. "Doc, you need to put some weight on those bones. I'm serious. You look like crap. And nobody calls me *Mister Perry*. It's Bud."

I looked helplessly to Kathryn, who could only wave limply as she tried to smother her laughter. Bud hobbled out to the front desk to pay his bill. I followed behind, scribbling a note, and reached for the phone behind the partition separating me from the checkout counter by all of six feet.

"Hello, this is Doctor Radis."

"Doctor, this is Gerald Tingley on Cliff Island. Mother's been having some trouble; wondered if you might come down the bay and look her over."

"Trouble?" I asked uneasily before committing myself more fully.

"Breathing trouble." Then, after a long pause, "Can't seem to catch her breath."

I closed my eyes, focusing, running my fingers through a shock of thinning light brown hair. Self-consciously, I felt the edge of my belt buckle and realized I was on the last notch. My pants draped loosely off my hips. I glanced at the mirror above the sink. I pulled down a lower eyelid, inspecting the conjunctiva for signs of anemia. Maybe I need some vitamins.

"Her breathing problem—did it start today?"

"Been this way since last week but got worse last night. The oxygen don't seem to be holding her. She's asking if you can make the trip, come out to Cliff Island, check her out, maybe switch out her pills."

Resting a foot on the edge of the metal three-drawer desk, I leaned back into my chair, listening, sorting out what to say next. Beyond the checkout counter was the waiting room. On the dull orange, threadbare carpet a toddler stacked blocks at the feet of a young mother, as several nuns, seated directly across, looked on. One nun was humming as she knitted. The other, a good eighty pounds over ideal body weight, grimaced as she shifted a swollen leg on a cushion; that would be Sister Mia.

To the right, adjacent to the waiting room, I could see a narrow alcove with a refrigerator and sink. To enter, one passed through swinging half-doors, saloon fashion. On the counter was an ancient microscope with brass fittings manufactured by the Bausch and Lomb optical company. Next to it was a package of microscope slides and coverslips, a bottle of immersion oil with a dropper, and a rack of smaller bottles required to perform a Gram stain—a series of stains enabling me to visualize bacteria, either gram-positive or gram-negative, when I focused the microscope on the highest magnification. Adjacent to the microscope was a centrifuge, a critical piece of equipment. After drawing blood and centrifuging the tubes, they would be refrigerated until I transported them to the hospital laboratory.

In the cabinets above the microscope were sterile containers for urine cultures, dipsticks to assess for blood or protein in the urine, throat and wound culture swabs, and a spare glucometer. A syringe prefilled with .3 cubic centimeters of one to one thousand epinephrine was taped to the inside of the cabinet door. If a patient suffered a severe anaphylactic reaction, injecting the epinephrine promptly might be the difference between life and death while the fireboat chugged out to Peaks. I liked the surety of the prefilled syringe; the last thing you want to do when a patient abruptly gasps for breath is track down where the epinephrine and syringe are located. Medications? Samples of antibiotics, blood pressure meds, and pain relievers were stored in a shelf adjacent to the hallway. Some patients had family members who could pick up prescriptions in town after work, but if not, it might be two or three days before a prescription arrived on the island from a pharmacy in Portland—an unacceptable wait.

Around the corner from the laboratory were two exam rooms. One was a bit larger than the other—my "procedure room," where I kept supplies for wound care and suturing and performed gynecologic exams. The other was cozier, with framed photos of animals and island scenes on the walls. This was our pediatric room.

All told, the Peaks Island Health Center measured, perhaps, thirty-five by twenty-five feet, making up the bottom story of a cottage donated to the island by a family who had lost a child to suicide.

In recent years, insulation has been blown in to the walls, the double-hung windows replaced on the ground floor, and a wooden ramp installed to improve access, but from the outside, if one were walking up Sterling Street, you'd never guess the cream-colored cottage was the home of the island's health center.

Kathryn reached around the divider and flashed me a note: *Portland police boat can be at Peaks Island dock: 40 minutes*. I mouthed the words *No house call* and shook my head emphatically; an elderly woman short of breath six miles off the coast needs an emergency room, not a house call.

"Mister Tingley—"

"Gerald be fine."

"Gerald—"

"Hold on there, Doc. Mother, you've got yourself tangled up but good. No wonder you're having such a time; tube's crimped under the chair. Lean forward; let me snake this 'round your neck. There. Now try to slow down your breathing. Doc, oxygen is on four."

"Gerald, listen to me carefully. I'm in the middle of clinic hours here on Peaks. Even if I did come out to Cliff Island later today, I can't properly evaluate your mother, much less treat her without a chest X-ray and blood work. We can arrange a transfer uptown in less than an hour and a half. I can meet her at the hospital later this evening—"

"Doc, I've moved to the kitchen; got to keep my voice down. We're having quite a time, I'd say quite a time, and the straight up is she's not coming into town. Said so when she got off the ferry last week."

"Mister Tingley, help me out here. Why is your mother on oxygen? What's wrong with her lungs?" I asked.

"Lung."

"Excuse me?"

"Lung. Only got one lung. Lung cancer. Surgery was in Philadelphia last month, where she lives when she's not summering on Cliff. The doctors say she's cured, but they had to take a lung. We thought she'd never get off the respirator. Pneumonia settled in, heart failure, the works."

I slouched down further in my swivel chair. "Gerald. Your mother absolutely has to be transferred to an emergency room. Now, which hospital do I tell the rescue boat she'll be coming to?"

There was a long pause. "Doc, she says she'd rather die here at home than go back to the hospital." He cleared his throat. "It's not a pretty sight; hard all the way 'round, if you take my meaning. My brother and me been up all night with her. Things are running kind of thin."

The sound of a woman's voice cut Gerald off, and the phone rattled to the floor. Then, silence.

"Doctor," Mrs. Tingley was on the line, her breathing coming in shallow, raspy gasps. "Doctor Radis, thank. You. For. Coming."

I heard myself telling her I was on my way as soon as the police boat arrived. Hanging up the phone, I grumbled to Kathryn there was no room in my bag for an emergency room. I should have stood firm: No House Call.

"You should see Sister Mia before you leave," Kathryn said. "She has an infection behind her heel. Sister Marie Henry is fine; she's here for support. I've already taken a throat swab on the little boy. It's positive for strep; we have liquid penicillin samples to get him started. I can call Rosemont Pharmacy for the remainder. With luck it'll be down on the 4:30 ferry. I'll call Sandi for you; she may need to hold your dinner. Do you have the spare oxygen tank and an extra IV setup? If something comes up, I'll reach you on your beeper."

Thirty minutes later, I straddled my three-speed Schwinn, the emergency box dangling off one handlebar and my green satchel off the other, strapped the spare oxygen tank onto the bike rack, and set off for the dock.

"Good morning, Doctor Radis!" An adolescent boy jogged past as I turned onto Island Avenue. "We have the day off from school," he shouted, briefly running backward. I tried to place him: carrot-mop hair, long legs, short torso. Had I seen him at the health center? I watched him disappear around the corner., compact stride, quick leg turnover. As a former college runner, I knew a budding talent when I saw one. Ricky . . . Ricky Hogan. Now I remembered. He'd mown our lawn twice this summer. Sandi'd said he could use the money. Nice kid; he'd played with our two-year-old, Kate, after finishing the lawn. Single mom. Dad . . . What had I heard? Absent.

I tested my brakes at Down Front, the local ice creamery, and rattled down the ancient cobblestones of Welch Street to the Peaks Island wharf.

The twenty-eight-foot *Connolly* glided into the dock at mid-tide. Exposed mussel flats shhhhh-ed as the wake of the boat sent a freshet of water farther up the beach. With his wraparound aviator glasses, Officer Bob Eldridge gave the heady impression that at any moment he might be called away for a crucial drug bust. In reality, he had the cushiest assignment on the force. Pushing off, he maneuvered the boat past several late-season moorings before throttling up the diesel and slicing through uneven chop into mid-channel. "Where we off to?"

"Cliff Island. Tingleys'."

"The Tingley boys' lobster." He seemed to be searching an internal database of island names and associations. A fog bank loomed ahead in the channel between Peaks and Long Island. Officer Bob removed his sunglasses and flipped on the radar screen and casually adjusted the settings. "Old Lady Tingley—I thought she died."

Not yet, I thought.

Underway, I opened my emergency tackle box, quietly reviewing my medications from A—albuterol inhaler, an asthmatic medication, to Z—Zaroxolyn, a potent diuretic that can quickly remove excess fluid. My Sears Bassmaster tackle box included several drugs I've never used outside the hospital setting. These are my what-if drugs. As in, *What if I am an hour from the hospital and a patient's asthma is life-threatening?* IV methylprednisolone and subcutaneous epinephrine are the answer. What if an islander becomes psychotic? Haldol. Heart attack? Subcutaneous heparin, aspirin, morphine. Or falls into a diabetic coma? Insulin and IV fluids. From a side pocket I pulled out my portable glucometer and checked the batteries. Everything seemed to be in working order.

House calls are a throwback to the time when medicine was more art than science, more intuition than definitive diagnosis, and not all of my house calls have been resounding successes. On my first house call last summer I'd forgotten to pack a thermometer, its significance heightened by my inability to simply stop rummaging through my black bag. I should have felt the patient's forehead and declared it felt a little warm instead of acting like a total imposter. Over time, though, I am developing a routine, a comfort zone.

No, this house call is out of my comfort zone. Way out.

The fog met us, blanketing the boat in a cool, white mist. Officer Bob cut our speed by half and adjusted the gain on the radar. He unbuttoned his collar, his face reflected in the green glow of the radar screen. A wave slapped the bow, and then another, the heavyset police boat rocking ever so slightly. Flipping the radar off and on, Officer Bob rechecked the chart and tapped the compass with his index finger. We slowed further. It felt wrong. He gave the horn three long blasts, a warning to nearby boats, and took off his cap before readjusting it a little lower over his eyes.

The wind shifted, and, as if touched by a magician's wand, the outline of Pumpkin Knob, an outcropping off the north end of Peaks Island materialized. Moments later we were in full sunlight, bouncing over shore-driven chop toward Cliff Island, five miles distant, the fog bank receding behind us like a great gray wall. Outside the shelter of the inner islands, the wind gusted a good fifteen to twenty knots, but the sky was a brilliant blue with an early September chill in the air. We scattered a raft of eiders, the chunkier black-and-white males (skunk ducks in the local parlance) beating their wings frantically to clear a line of white caps.

Coming into Cliff in the lee of the wind, we maneuvered past the dilapidated main pier to the inside of a rectangular float where dinghies were tied like horses at a hitching post. I clambered out on the bow of the police boat with a paddle, pushed aside a dinghy, and jumped onto the float. Officer Eldridge handed me my black bag, the spare oxygen tank, and house call tackle box. I stared at the iron-rung ladder hanging off the pier, tucked the tank under an arm, and tied the tackle box to my belt before ascending, one-handed. Then I retrieved my black bag.

No one said it would be easy.

Above us, on the main pier, a gaunt, bearded man in a faded blue windbreaker silently watched my progress. As I pushed open the gate at the top of the ladder, he extended a hand.

"She's not great, but that extra fluid pill you told me to give Mother seemed to do the trick—that, and turning up the oxygen a dite. Gerald Tingley." He leaned out over the gate and shouted down to officer Eldridge. "Hey, Bobbi, want to come out to the house?" Bob waved him off and opened up the newspaper.

I was tight as a bowstring, reviewing my what-ifs. Shoot, I realized, I'd forgotten the blood-draw kit. What if I needed to draw blood? Maybe I had a spare kit wrapped in with my reflex hammer and tuning fork. No, it doesn't matter. No need to draw blood; she's coming to town. Period.

We climbed into Gerald's ancient Dodge pickup, the corroded bed covered by two sheets of plywood. Rust had claimed the wheel wells and worked its way back toward the tailgate. A twisted piece of oak driftwood served as a bumper. The engine caught and sputtered, stalled. I fumbled instinctively for my seat belt before realizing the truck not only lacked this rudimentary feature but also had no directional signal, emergency brake, radio, inspection sticker, or windshield wipers.

Curious about the heater, I asked Gerald if it ran. "Like a pip." He flipped the blower on, and my baseball cap flipped off. "Just the basics," he grinned. "Most of the trucks and cars on Cliff couldn't get stickered in town, so they wound up here instead of a junk pile. Elephant's graveyard."

Traveling down a narrow dirt road, away from the bay, deeper into red spruce and lowbush blueberry, I closed my eyes and tried to relax and enjoy the scenery. Out of the wind, late morning sunshine warmed the cab as we drove by fading patches of chicory and rose hips and tangled clumps of Queen Anne's lace. Above us a canopy of sugar maple interwoven with stands of spruce and white pine glided by. The muffled sound of surf on a cobblestone beach reached us over the drone of the muffler-less Dodge. Gerald pulled over and cut the engine.

"Grab your stuff, Doc."

Okay, I thought, this is it. Placing my Littmann stethoscope around my neck like a talisman, I patted my cowlick down and gave myself a pep talk: Here we go. Be sharp. But from the roadside there was no house, only unbroken forest.

"The house is down this way, out on the point." Gerald pointed to a narrow dirt path leading into the woods.

I dutifully followed, lugging my supplies into the cool darkness. The path wound around bare outcroppings of ledge and stands of stunted red spruce, their low-lying branches draping over the trail. "How in the world did your mother get to the house?" I asked.

"Walked," Gerald replied.

"Isn't there another entrance—a roadway, some type of shortcut?"

"Trail don't usually bother her; reminds her of a fairy tale. I usually clean the trail out once or twice a year." He paused. "To be truthful, I didn't think she'd be back this fall."

I heard the surf long before we emerged from the forest. Stopping at the edge of an overgrown meadow, we watched shoulder-high rollers explode onto exposed bedrock, sending geyser-like plumes of spray skyward. On the point, a weather-beaten, brown-shingled cottage faced the open ocean. A shallow porch with a sagging roofline extended from the water side. Across the reach, perhaps three-fourths of a mile distant, was Jewell Island, beyond it the Gulf of Maine.

Reaching the porch, I gripped my black doctor bag tightly and opened the screen door. Inside, Mrs. Tingley, all ninety pounds of her, looked even worse than I'd expected. Slumped in a wooden rocker, her blue eyes focused on an indefinite point beyond the breakers, her breathing came in irregular, shallow, bird-like gasps. Another son, stockier and shorter by a head than Gerald, fidgeted with her oxygen tube and managed to shake his head hopelessly.

I laid my hand on Mrs. Tingley's shoulder and told her without much conviction that she was going to be okay. On the sofa behind her, I opened the tackle box, the three trays on each side unfolding like a flowering rose, exposing my therapeutic options. The two brothers stood off to one side, waiting.

I listened briefly to the right lung—or rather the former site of the right lung. Silence. Inching my stethoscope around to the left lung, I auscultated a racing, chaotic heart rhythm amid a background of high-pitched wheezes and crackles. I placed my stethoscope on the chest again and palpated her pulse at the wrist. The rhythm was definitely an irregular irregularity. The diagnosis: atrial fibrillation with congestive heart failure, or, in a more descriptive, bygone era, dropsy.

Glancing down at my watch, I counted the heart rate over fifteen seconds and then multiplied this by four: 160 per minute. I wrote this down in my pocket calendar and continued my exam. Her fingertips were a dusky blue, her lower legs massively swollen. When I pressed with my index finger into the soft tissues around the ankles, it left a persistent indentation.

Her heart rhythm—atrial fibrillation—was responsible for her rapid decline. As the heart races, fluid backs up and spills out into the lungs and soft tissues. Less oxygen leads to further pump failure and, inevitably, a slow-motion, drowning death. It's a hard way to go. No wonder the brothers had wanted me to come; it's tough watching a loved one drown.

I reached for a vial of digitalis and, as I drew it up, realized we might have passed foxglove, the original plant source, on our walk through the field. Digitalis strengthens the pumping motion of the heart and will slow the irregular, racing rhythm of atrial fibrillation, but I'd never before given it outside the hospital setting. Give the proper dose, and the heart responds; infuse too much, and it acts as a toxin. In medical parlance, digitalis has a "narrow therapeutic window." I broke open a vial and slowly injected one-fourth milligram, wrote down the dosage and time, and waited.

"Mrs. Tingley," I squatted down in front of her rocking chair. "Mrs. Tingley?" She looked up vacantly, as if seeing me for the first time. "I'm afraid I need to insist you come into town. The police boat is waiting."

She clasped my hand lightly. "Thank. You. For. Coming."

I took that as a yes. We'd make the transfer, but first Mrs. Tingley had to be stabilized. If she decompensated on the trail. . . . Well, I pushed that thought aside. Focus. Concentrate on the present. During the next hour and a half, I drew up and injected several additional doses of digitalis along with furosemide, a potent diuretic.

Gerald moved a bedside commode next to the rocker, and the boys lifted her onto it when their mother felt an overwhelming urge to urinate. Three times she relieved herself, only to nod off, slumping forward, when she returned to the rocker. By midafternoon, her heart and respiratory rate were halved, the coarse, rattling congestion of her lung replaced by a Buddha-like serenity.

Pulling a strand of matted hair behind her ear, she looked at me as if for the first time. "Thought you were going to lose me, didn't you?"

"Your lungs—I mean, lung—is clearer now," I answered. "Yes, you were close. You can't stay here tonight."

"It's an awful feeling, not getting enough air," she replied. "I felt like I was in the water. Warm milk was all around me, and I couldn't see." She cleared her throat. "Alright, I'm back in the lifeboat," she said firmly. "Gerald, get my cane." She rose abruptly and took a step toward the screen door.

"Mother! Hold on! Wait!" Gerald grabbed the oxygen tank. Mrs. Tingley's doughy legs suddenly crumpled, and she allowed herself to collapse back into the rocking chair, rivulets of sweat soaking her nightgown.

It was Gerald who suggested we transport his mother in the rocking chair. There was no other way. The brothers hoisted the chair onto their broad shoulders while I assumed the lead, carrying the portable oxygen tank. Through the open field we marched in royal procession while I struggled to maintain the proper distance: Too far ahead and the oxygen tube pulled at her nose like a ring on a bull's nose, too close and the trailing cord threatened to trip up our entourage. I mulled over the treatment she'd received and decided nothing more could be done to stabilize her for the transfer to town.

At the edge of the meadow, Mrs. Tingley looked back, straining, for one last glimpse of the cottage before we entered the woods, then, THWACK! A low-lying branch sprung back against her face. The brothers wobbled uncertainly as a shower of spruce needles rained down. Panicking, I compounded the problem by stretching the oxygen line, and Mrs. Tingley's head lurched forward. The two men attempted to right the load.

"Lower!" Mrs. Tingley gasped. "Lower!" Duckwalking, their knees nearly bumping their chests, the men pushed on. "My nose! Watch my nose!" Too late, the tube whipped off her nose onto an adjacent spruce branch, oxygen hissing from the free end.

The men backed out from beneath the rocker, somehow changing their grip to the outside rail, and lowered their mother gently to the trail. In the thirty seconds it had taken for me to retrieve the oxygen tube and place it back on her nose, her fingers had turned a pallid blue-black. This time I taped the tube to her cheek and pinned a loop to her wool sweater. Better to pull off a swath of cloth than lose the oxygen again.

Gerald smoked a cigarette and wiped the back of his bloodstained hand against his trousers. We sat on a moss-covered log, reviewing our options.

"No way we can drag the chair on the trail." Gerald said. "She'd 'bout come undone."

"It's not too far," I said finally. We all knew that was a lie. Gerald looked at his cigarette and stubbed it out on a tree root. We soon found that if I walked backward, facing Mrs. Tingley, I could control the tension on the oxygen tube. To free up my hands, I placed the emergency kit on her lap and dangled my doctor's bag off an arm of the rocker.

Mrs. Tingley, for her part, assumed the role of scout, guiding me against the vagaries of the trail. The men were blind. Bent like beasts of burden, they could see no further ahead than their boot tops. There was no grumbling; if there is a gene for willful stubbornness, she had passed it on to the boys.

"To the left," she rasped. I scuffed an elbow against a wind-scoured boulder. "Lower!" Mrs. Tingley flailed at the understory. Somehow the men stooped even lower. "Lift your feet!" I tripped and caught myself by flinging an arm around a sapling. On the rebound, Gerald caught the sapling square in the face, grunted an obscenity, and held on.

Reaching the road, the brothers lowered the rocker while I reexamined Mrs. Tingley. Her heart rate held steady at a reasonable ninety beats per minute. The digoxin had done its job. Breath sounds in her remaining lung were moist with crackles in the lower portion but clearer in the upper portions. A superficial scrape across her forehead was the only evidence of her harrowing journey through the woods.

Gerald lit another cigarette and leaned against the truck. He handed the cigarette to his brother, who took two nervous puffs, coughed, and licked his fingers before snuffing out the cigarette between his thumb and forefinger.

Three monarch butterflies fluttered erratically about, drawing nourishment from late-season goldenrod and milkweed before launching improbably across the sound toward Mexico, two thousand miles to the southwest. Their movement caught Mrs. Tingley's eye, and she silently followed their graceful dance until they disappeared across the meadow. Only then did the two brothers load their mother onto the truck bed.

Tight against the cab, she faced the rear bumper, straight-backed, emotionless. The boys clambered up and stood on each side of the rocker. Gerald brushed a pine twig out of her hair and reached up with his shirttail to wipe a smudge off her cheek. He knocked on the window. I started the truck.

Like phantoms, island neighbors drifted to the roadside. I drove as if I were leading a funeral procession for the living, no faster than a slow amble, stopping once for an elderly woman who motioned me over and, clasping Mrs. Tingley's hand, left a faded blue aster in her palm. By the time we reached the dock, there were eighteen in the entourage.

Officer Bob folded his newspaper as he saw us backing down the wharf. He steadied the front of the rocker as we transferred Mrs. Tingley aboard the *Connolly* and placed her on the diesel cowling—a flat, elevated platform at midship outside the cabin. The boys reluctantly cast off. Underway, a fine mist played over the water. Mrs. Tingley faced astern, a solitary figurehead, the crowd on the dock growing smaller and smaller until we rounded the point.

CHAPTER TWO

I knew I couldn't live in America, and I wasn't ready to
move to Europe, so I moved to an island off the coast of
America.

—Spalding Gray

Few bays in the world are blessed with the concentration of islands
as Casco Bay. Within the body of water between Small Point in
Harpswell and the tip of Cape Elizabeth twenty-six miles distant, there are either 220 or 138 islands, depending on how one defines
an island. The larger number includes bridged islands, upriver islands
bathed in tidal flow, barren ledges exposed during tidal cycles, and
twinned islands emerging during the highest tides. The smaller number
reflects the opinion that a "true" island must be reached by boat and is
sufficiently above the tides that vegetation gains a permanent foothold.

There are so many islands in Casco Bay that four are named Crow.
There is a Goose Island, a cluster of Goslings, an Eagle, and a Horse.
There were formerly two Hog Islands until wealthy summer residents
grew weary of this association and rechristened them Little and Great
Diamond Islands. If you hold a nautical chart just so, Basket Island
does resemble a basket and Crab a crab. There are birches on Birch
Island and deer on Deer.

Bustins Island and Cushing Island are summer islands, bursting
with energy five months of the year and fallow for seven. Some islands
have been owned by a single family for generations. Another fourteen
are town- or state-owned. But the rarest of them all are the year-round
island communities where children attend an island school. Out of
an estimated four thousand islands along Maine's rocky coast, fourteen meet this definition. Four of them are in Casco Bay: Cliff Island,

population seventy-one; Long Island, population 237; Chebeague Island, population 341; and Peaks Island, population 840.

What led me to practice medicine on the year-round islands in Casco Bay? Let's say that there were a lot of moving parts—that and equal measures of luck, persistence, hubris, and naivete.

As a medical student at the Kansas City University of Medicine and Bioscience I was awarded a National Health Service Corps Scholarship. In return for each year of free tuition, I promised to practice a year in what the federal government called a US "health manpower-shortage area." Some of my classmates were assigned to remote clinics in Idaho or Montana or West Virginia. Another family made the eastern Arizona White Mountain Apache Tribe reservation their new home. New sites were added to serve inner-city residents in Newark, Detroit, and LA.

It was well into my second year of an internal medicine residency at the Osteopathic Hospital of Maine in the coastal city of Portland, Maine's largest city, that I kept bumping up against a curious reality: very few islanders landing in our emergency room laid claim to a primary care physician. With disturbing regularity, they presented with undiagnosed or undertreated ailments: diabetes, depression, peptic ulcer disease, emphysema, hypertension—you name it. With a little digging, I discovered that the only health clinic in the bay was on Peaks Island, and it was open only two half days a week. None of the other islands was served by a doctor.

In the ER—where I honed my primitive skills in suturing—on the medical floors, and in the intensive care unit, I found that islanders were plainspoken, hardheaded, and resilient. And they were a royal pain in the butt. They should have died—but almost never did. Once they were brought back from death's door, they demanded to be discharged. If it was critical that they complete a week of IV antibiotics in the hospital for life-threatening pneumonia, islanders were often dressed and ready to go home the morning of the fourth day. Despite the admonitions of my attending, they frequently signed out against medical advice. To be truthful, for some islanders I know this was the pull of substance abuse. Every day without alcohol or cigarettes—or, in more recent years, narcotics—was a losing battle with addiction.

More often, though, particularly with elderly islanders, their greatest fear was that they would be transferred to a rehab facility or a nursing home on the mainland. The islands were familiar and supportive; the mainland was foreign and unfeeling, a place where people told you what to do and when to do it. Islanders left AMA because they feared they would lose their independence.

I got that.

Curious, one day I purchased a map of Casco Bay and after dinner spread it out on our kitchen table. Hand-in-hand with information from the US census, I verified the year-round populations of Peaks, Long, Chebeague, and Cliff and learned that ferries traveled regularly to them. That night, I taped the map up in a side room. Soon there was a second yellow-lined paper taped to the wall with a list of questions:

- Can the islands, if they band together, qualify as a health manpower–shortage area?
- Can they still qualify if Doctor Kenney continues his part-time practice on Peaks Island?
- Is it too late to apply for federal designation?
- What do the islanders need to do to support the application?
- How will I get paid?

My wife, Sandi, and I didn't dread the payback or isolation of island life. Sandi was raised on a dairy farm in New Hampshire with dozens of round-faced Finnish relatives nearby. She'd grown up sewing many of her own clothes. Entertainment revolved around family social gatherings. Every Friday night neighbors flocked to Sandi's farmhouse for sauna, where they danced and drank and baked themselves deep into Saturday morning.

In the early years of our marriage, Sandi had worked a tough job, trying to change the trajectory of emotionally disturbed preschoolers at a therapeutic nursery run by Maine Medical Center psychiatry. But this was nothing out of the ordinary for the women in her family. Sandi's mom, Jeanne Korpela, and Aunt Amy were social workers; Sandi's sister and her sister's daughter and nephew were social workers. Sandi became a social worker. Looking back now, I can see that most of the Korpela women picked flawed men who were hard workers. When Sandi was age twenty-one, she picked me.

Though I'd grown up in suburban New Jersey, I gravitated toward fishing and camping and hiking. The Rahway River flowed through my hometown of Cranford (generously nicknamed the Venice of New Jersey), and my earliest memories are of wading in the rifles, turning over rocks, searching for crayfish. My mom, Shirley, watched from the embankment in her fold-up chair. As I wandered downstream, she would periodically pick up her chair to keep me in sight. The swath of forest separating the river from the congestion of New York City, twenty miles distant, was wide enough to slow time down.

After my father died when I was eleven, I didn't have much adult supervision and spent countless early mornings on the river. I kept my fly rod in my locker in junior high, but I wasn't fussy, fishing with whatever the fish were biting on: worms, streamers, store-bought salmon eggs, dry flies, bits of cheese. One summer in junior high my friend Tux and I built a raft, intent on floating the river to who knows where, maybe the Mississippi, but abandoned this soon after realizing the number of dams we'd need to traverse. Although we set traps, we never did successfully trap a muskrat.

Before my dad died, my favorite book had been C in *Compton's Encyclopedia*. Afterward, I drifted through high school and into college. I had friends; that probably saved me. My interest in medicine flowed from a chance meeting with a family doctor in Baja, Mexico. He was a DO, a doctor of osteopathic medicine. I was attracted to the philosophy of the profession; I liked the idea of treating the whole person. So I began to apply myself.

Not to say that the rest was easy. In my senior year of college, I met with the dean of students for Bates College, Doctor Carrigan, and announced my intention to apply to medical school. He looked at my grades from the first two years of college and raised an eyebrow. Then he reviewed my last two years of A's. "You know, Chuck," he said, patting me on the shoulder, "I've got to tell you, that ship has sailed."

Except that it hadn't. I did well on the Medical College Admission Test, and the Kansas City University of Medicine and Bioscience admitted me, I suspect more on the strength of my trajectory and potential than actual performance. Of course it didn't hurt that an article I had written on osteopathic medicine was published by a regional magazine.

As I explored whether the islands might be interested in working together for federal designation, the name Johanna von Tiling—pronounced "Yohanna"—kept coming up. So, one evening, I called her. After listening to my proposal on the phone, she was not particularly encouraging or optimistic but arranged for me to present my ideas at a meeting of Cliff Islanders.

That was how it started.

Then it nearly ended before it started. I mixed up the ferry departure times and missed the down-the-bay ferry to Cliff Island. Okay, it was even worse than that; I'd stopped at the YMCA on my way to the ferry and lost track of time, playing pickup basketball, and missed the boat. Fifty islanders sat in an unheated community hall for an hour waiting for me. There were no cell phones in those days. I called Johanna's home number three days straight before, in desperation, I wrote her a postcard. A week later I received an enigmatic reply: *March 10th, 5:45 ferry. You're either on the boat or off the boat.*

The *Island Romance* glided up to the Cliff Island wharf in silky darkness. From my perch behind the smokestack I could see the tailgate of a pickup piled high with lobster traps silhouetted by the light of a single streetlight. Snow dusted the traps and lay heavily against the far edge of the wharf. A deck hand gathered several coils of mooring line and heaved the mass of rope toward the wharf, where it dropped cleanly onto a cleat. From the warm belly of the *Island Romance*, only seven passengers remained from the seventy-five who'd boarded in Portland more than an hour ago. This was the end of the line. Those who filed out wearily gathered newspapers and packages, groceries, lunch pails, and empty beer bottles. Two deckhands helped a woman pick up a stroller with a toddler asleep inside and carried it over the gangplank.

On the lee side of the freight shed was Johanna von Tiling. She waved me over, stood back, and looked me over. Gray-eyed and sturdily built, with delicate wire-rimmed glasses and shoulder-length gray hair twisted into a tight bun, she had the no-nonsense presence of a schoolmarm. Which she was.

"Doctor Radis, we've got quite a crowd. There must be fifty or so, same as last time. Hurry—the meeting hall is on up this way." Then she turned away without another word. The *Island Romance* surged from the dock, the back wake rolling heavily against the wharf pilings, dislodging a slushy mixture of ice. In the few moments I'd taken to admire the receding outline of the ferry, the dock emptied. I grabbed my backpack and jogged up to the crossroads where Johanna waited impatiently.

Our heads bowed to the wind, snow stinging my eyes, I peppered Johanna with questions. "You'll find out soon enough," she answered stiffly, pulling her greatcoat tighter. I looked back. Our tracks leading from the wharf were already filling in.

Stepping inside the white clapboard Cliff Island community center a few minutes later, I was keenly aware of a steady drip-drip off my defrosting mustache as I shook hands with a man named Al, who wore a red mackinaw shirt and was built like a fire hydrant. Before me, backs turned, sat most of Cliff Island's year-round population.

Johanna, taking a seat in the rear, motioned me toward the front where a man wearing a faded army fatigue jacket and sporting a bucket-sized jet-black beard sat behind a card table, gavel in hand.

"We all know why we're here tonight," he began. "Doctor Radis, here, sit down." I took a seat. "Doctor Radis has come down tonight from Portland to talk with us about being our doctor—or at least seeing if he can get the federal government to allow him to be our doctor. It's all kind of confusing to me. Why don't I let him tell us what this is all about? Doctor Radis?"

I sat, holding my carefully prepared notes. I've been told it helps to find a friendly face to focus on when addressing strangers. I smiled weakly at Johanna, who made a stern, shooing motion to cut the nonsense and start talking. I cleared my throat. "Thank you, and thanks for coming out tonight."

"Stand up," the moderator insisted.

"What?"

"Stand up. People in the back want to see you."

"Oh, sure." I stood up. I could feel the collective eyes of the community size me up. Average height: Five feet, ten inches. Weight, 155 pounds. Bowlegged, prematurely thinning straw hair, blond-gray peppered mustache, optimistic brown eyes. I wondered if they wanted to see my coffee-stained teeth. "Perhaps you can make the best sense of the proposal I'm bringing before you if I outline just what the National Health Service Corps is and why Cliff Island may benefit." A woman in the front row smiled. I felt my shoulders relax.

"Six and a half years ago, when I entered medical school, I joined the National Health Service Corps. After finishing my residency, I promised to serve in what is called a *health manpower–shortage area*, a town that fulfills certain criteria—chief among them the absence of regular medical care. If there is sufficient interest, I want to work with you to achieve that designation. I'd like to know firsthand, is there a need for a physician to make regular visits to Cliff Island?"

"Old Lady Milliken—she's nearly bedbound, isn't she, Ruth?" It was fireplug Al, who stood to make his comment. Ruth agreed a house call now and then would do Old Lady Milliken a world of good.

"Doctor Radis, what do you mean by 'regular visits,'" asked the young woman in the front row with the welcoming smile. "I mean, if one of my kids has a sore throat, are you going to take a round-trip ferry of three hours to see him? And between the islands, if you were at the clinic on Peaks, you'd have to go all the way back to Portland and catch another boat out to Cliff Island. You'd spend half your day seeing one patient."

"Well, to tell you the truth," I replied, "tonight was my first experience with the ferry." There was a soft murmur of good-natured snickering from the crowd. "But, no. Realistically, I don't think I could break up my day if I were seeing patients on another island, unless it were an emergency."

"Doctor Radis," Johanna spoke up, "we don't schedule our sicknesses out here. Now emergencies, that's another matter. Every time the fireboat chugs out here from Portland, it's over two hours between when we make the call until we arrive at the hospital. It makes sense that if we needed stitches or the like we could hold on until a doctor arrived."

"You call stitches emergencies, Johanna?" Al piped up. There was an edge to his voice. "When's the last time anybody called the fireboat for stitches? Lobster boat can take anyone in for stitches. That's no emergency. Doctor Pritkin here can help with deciding about all that anyway, can't you, Doc?"

Now this was interesting. Maybe this whole idea was a waste of time. Johanna hadn't mentioned anything about a doctor living on Cliff Island. But there he was, right out of a Norman Rockwell painting, silver-haired, crew cut, ruddy cheeked, a pipe set in the corner of his mouth. He tamped down the unlit pipe and clasped his hands behind his head.

"Al, I've said this before, and I'll say it again. I'm retired. Not only that, but I don't even have a medical license to practice anymore. Let's hear this young man out. Anybody notice that most of us are getting along in years? I might need him myself; you never know."

"Well, maybe we will, and maybe we won't," Al replied, unconvinced. "I do know if we had a real emergency, like someone was cutting wood and—*Whoosh!*—one arm was lopped off, I could call Naval Air Station Brunswick, and they'd land a chopper on the upper field, and we'd be off to Maine Medical Center in nothing flat."

"Hold on, hold on," Johanna shouted out. "Now, I'll have you all know there is no way the Brunswick Naval Air Station will ever send a helicopter down the bay. Have they ever done it? No! I've checked. I've called."

"Johanna, when did you call? Five, ten years ago?" Al shot back. "Or don't you remember? Things getting a little fuzzy, are they?"

"Why, you fat little wimp!" Johanna stood and waded through two rows of Cliff Islanders, arms raised, fists cocked. "Emergency or no emergency, I'm telling you, no helicopter will fly out to Cliff Island."

"Johanna! Al! Both of you, sit down!" Our moderator pounded his gavel. "*Hey! I said sit down!*" Johanna and Al's heads snapped to attention. The veins on the side of our moderator's temples looked like they would explode. Johanna and Al took their seats.

"We've got a lot of ground to cover tonight," the moderator glowered. "And while the emergency-system issues that Al and Johanna have raised are important, let's move on. Doctor Radis."

I cleared my throat and tried to think of a bland, non-life-threatening remark. "In the coming months, I'll be going to other year-round islands—Long, Chebeague, and Peaks Islands—to gather information. Individually, none of you has the year-round population to qualify for the program; only by working together will this come about . . . if you want it to come about."

"Now, Long and Chebeague, I can understand them being in on this plan," the moderator said. "But Peaks? Half the people work in Portland. That's a city island." The crowd grumbled in agreement.

"No, that's where you have it wrong," I persisted. "The federal government is very clear on this." I opened up my copy of the federal application. "A health manpower–shortage area must have, at a minimum, eighteen hundred year-round residents. Individually Cliff, Long, Chebeague, and Peaks don't even come close. By adding summer residents as one-half full-time equivalents and banding together you might qualify. There's no question, Peaks must be included in any plan for federal designation of Casco Bay."

"Now, there's something I can finally agree with the Feds on," Doc Pritkin said. "Anybody who considers summer people one-half full-time equivalents is okay by me. Next time that snooty Massachusetts couple tries to cut in line again down front, we'll just set 'em straight on who the full-time equivalents on this island are."

That did it. If there were a more popular target for trashing among Cliff Islanders than Peaks Island, it was the entitled summer resident. Sensing this, I made my final point. "Now, this isn't going to just happen. If it's something you want, then I'd like to work with you and make it happen. What do I need? Only support for the concept and letters to the federal agency administering the program. They need to know the kind of hardships you folks go through for routine and emergency care. The rest, well, the rest will depend on what you want and what I can give. Any other questions?

"We've got to wrap this up, everybody," our moderator interjected. "Sounds like we've got some information to chew on. Doctor Radis, thanks for coming out, I'm sure everyone appreciates it. We've still got the septic system problem and the spring ferry schedule to talk about. We'll take one more question. Al?"

Drawing himself up slowly and deliberately, Al jabbed a finger at Johanna. "Now, about that helicopter!"

Amid the ensuing shouts and accusations, I grabbed my coat and slipped outside.

Long Island was next. By now I'd grown accustomed to reading the ferry schedule. Though Peaks and Long Islands were less than a half mile apart, they were serviced by different ferries. The *Island Romance* ran down the bay, stopping at Little and Great Diamond, Long, Chebeague, and Cliff Islands, while the *Machigonne* was dedicated to the more frequent twenty-minute trips between Peaks Island and Portland.

On the first warm day of early spring, I picked a Sunday afternoon for the forty-minute ferry to Long Island. My meeting on Cliff, strange as it was, had been curiously productive, yielding more than a dozen letters supporting designation by the federal government. Johanna von Tiling and I now spoke regularly about deadlines and strategy. Despite her prickliness, I'd lucked out with the right contact person for Cliff Island.

The *Island Romance* idled down as it approached Long Island. A dozen or so lobster boats bobbed on their moorings. (No lobstering is permitted in Maine on Sundays during the summer months). A stooped elderly man limped to the edge of the wharf and shouted, "Where's my goddamn tombstone?"

The word came down from the pilothouse, "next boat."

"That's what you jokers said last Sunday and the Sunday afore that. What kind of outfit you boys runnin' these days?" the man shot back, clenching his fists. "Mother wanted a headstone, that's all I know. She was particular 'bout it. 'Don't you scatter me like a bag of coal dust; bury me proper.' She must've said it a dozen times."

The captain leaned out of the pilothouse. "Give it up, Fred. We'll get your stone soon enough." Fred turned abruptly and slammed the door of his pickup and drove off the wharf.

Carl Thompson stepped forward and patted my shoulder. "Don't worry yourself, doctor. Fred'll play out soon enough. Can't say I blame him; that stone's been gathering dust and grime in the freight shed in Portland for weeks. Best we get a move on; it's a fifteen-minute walk to the house." He checked his watch. "We've got seven ladies waiting for you. My god, they've got a million questions."

Along the road we passed a line of weathered cottages perched on the bay, each served by an outhaul where a dinghy or pleasure boat was moored offshore. A stretch of chain-link fence ran parallel to the road on the inland side, and behind this was an open field. Sensing my interest, Carl pointed to the fence. "Government property during World War II; now some outfit from Texas bought it a few years back. Buried somewhere behind that fence are underground tanks big enough to fuel an aircraft carrier. Can you imagine? A line of wharfs nine hundred feet long off Long Island with a destroyer or aircraft carrier fueling up each side. They stacked the North Atlantic fleet in here tighter than salted cod in a barrel. Now it's as if the war never happened. Forty years is enough to wipe the slate clean. Only thing that lasts is stone, you know."

Turning inland, we passed old-growth oak and maple and stands of white birch before arriving at a south-facing cottage and an attached barn set in a clearing. Carl and I entered through the mudroom and, after introducing me to his wife, Libby, sheepishly admitted that he didn't care much for meetings and retreated to his small engine-repair shop.

Libby shook my hand enthusiastically and introduced me to her "ad hoc committee." Tea and a delicious assortment of crumb cake, apple turnovers, and blueberry muffins was passed around the table. "I've been talking to Johanna from Cliff Island, and she said that the meeting was one of their most exciting in years," Libby began.

"Well, I'll have to follow up with her soon," I replied. "That's great. The other islands in the bay seem to be interested in designation too."

"Oh, speaking of that, Blanchard Bates called yesterday. I understand he's hosting an evening meeting for Chebeague Island later this month and is counting on you to join them."

"Of course, Blanchard Bates"—I had no idea who he was. "You wouldn't happen to have Mister Bates's phone number, would you?"

I plucked my At-a-Glance pocket calendar from my shirt pocket and wrote down the number as she recited it from memory. Patting my back pocket, I realized I didn't have my wallet. Dang.

"Now, let's get down to business. Before you came, Doctor Radis, we were discussing where you could see patients. Jane suggested we add a twelve-by-twelve addition to the grade school."

The wallet wasn't in my other back pocket. I retraced my morning. I had no idea where my wallet was.

"We think Jane might be on to something. What do you think, Doctor Radis?"

I blinked, processing what Libby had said. "That would be great—just big enough for an exam table and supplies. On Peaks Island," I added, "a small cottage was donated to the island to serve as a clinic." There. I was proving that I knew something useful about the islands of Casco Bay.

"Where would the money come from if we built the addition?" Libby asked the group, skipping over my comment.

I wondered if I needed money for anything today. I was almost positive that my ticket I'd handed to the deckhand for the ferry to Long Island had been round-trip. If not? Borrowing money from people I've just met didn't seem to be a good way to build trust and confidence in their future physician. Then it came to me: my wallet was in the pants I'd worn yesterday, on the hook, in the closet. Good—that was sort of progress. I rejoined the conversation. "On Peaks Island," I interrupted the conversation, "I'm told the community raised two thousand dollars for an EKG machine and an exam table through a library book sale."

I was oblivious to the cool breeze. Several of the women frowned. Libby continued. "On the other hand, part of the reason for this meeting is to brainstorm with Doctor Radis. I don't have any doubt that we can raise the money for an addition on the school. Perhaps the bigger focus should be on house calls. With only two hundred or so of us in the winter, it would be a blessing to have our elderly seen in their homes. And we should think about improving our emergency capabilities."

"I was thinking the same thing," I added. "The Portland police department has offered to transport me between the islands on their boat. So that will help. As far as improving emergency services, do you have a policeman on the island? On Peaks Island the police are triple trained in law enforcement and firefighting and as emergency medical technicians. It's amazing that—"

"Doctor Radis," Libby cut me off. Her teacup hung in midair, pinky out. "Frankly, we don't give a shi t what they do on Peaks Island. Their men came over, dead of night, and cut our lobster pot lines not a hundred yards off shore from Vail Island, and Vail, as everyone knows," she said, looking soberly from face to face around the table, "has always been Long Island lobstering grounds."

I shrunk back into my chair.

Carl piped up from the kitchen: "Course, a lot of them boys are gone now, Libby. That was some years ago. Peaks has changed. You can count on one hand the number of lobstermen on Peaks: Bobby Spear, Covey Johnson, Bob Emerson. They tell me they've got 150 commuters on their 7:15 morning ferry all dressed up like bankers and lawyers. It's a rich man's island."

I chose my words carefully. "This meeting is a first step in assessing Long Island's special needs and priorities, but each island needs to be included in the application for the federal government to take this proposal seriously."

"We've heard about those full-time and half-time equivalents," Libby said thickly. "That's why we're here. We want in, just as long as Peaks Island doesn't get too big a piece of the pie."

A few minutes later, Carl joined me in the mudroom while I glumly pulled on my boots. He squeezed my shoulder. "Doc, gotta get some thicker skin if you're gonna play with this bunch. But I've got a hunch that this medical business just might stumble forward."

I nodded, saying nothing.

"The *Island Romance* be coming along soon," Carl said. "This time of year, if you're not waitin' on the wharf, they might just cruise by kind of slow. Saves them a few minutes of tying up for nobody in particular."

Despite my bumbling, a number of letters supporting designation for the Casco Bay islands trickled in from Long Island. I caught the *Island Romance* for a second visit to Long Island a few weeks later, stopping in to see Bob and Nancy Jordan living off-the-grid in a passive-solar log home. The less-formal setting was far more comfortable and productive. For the first and only time I was asked, "Why in the world are you putting all this work into the islands?"

"To be honest, sometimes I don't know myself," I replied. "But the reason why I haven't taken the easier path and taken a job in an established clinic is that I've been looking for the right fit. I've never lived on an island, but by and large, when I'm talking with islanders, and treating islanders at my hospital, I feel like they're my people. I admire toughness and stubbornness—maybe even a little craziness and eccentricity. So why not see where it goes?"

My new friends living off-grid understood. It was the exact same reason they'd moved to Long Island.

A few weeks later, Sandi and I, with Kate in tow, boarded the *Machigonne* ferry for the twenty-minute ride to Peaks Island. Sandi remained skeptical but open-minded about an island medical practice. She was already assessing how difficult it might be to live on Peaks and work in Portland. Childcare would be critical. A parking spot close to the ferry was important. Was housing affordable on the islands? I saw it as a good sign when she called her coworker Ellen, who lived on Peaks, to hear firsthand about island culture.

Ellen provided some key advice: If possible, avoid community meetings of any kind. If two islanders meet, there are three arguments. Gather support for federal designation by talking with individual islanders rather than with, say, the board of directors of the Peaks Island Health Center.

"Do you think your hours will be better once you finish the residency?" Sandi asked on board the *Machigonne*.

I squeezed her hand. "Got to be. For one thing, I should be more in charge of my hours." (What I didn't tell Sandi was the reaction of my program director, Phil Slocum, at the Osteopathic Hospital. When he'd heard that I intended to set up an island practice, he'd said, "If someone could scratch out a living on the islands, they'd already have a doctor. I hope your salary is guaranteed. If not, be ready to starve.")

"Better hours. I like that." With one finger she readjusted her glasses, her rounded cheeks accented with a dab of pink where the metal frames touched.

As we slowed to dock, I noticed that the Welcome to Peaks Island sign over the wharf had been altered, with the P crossed out and the letters Fr painted in freehand. As we filed off, everyone seemed to be lugging something to shore—bags of groceries in wheeled carts, lamps, flats of tomato seedlings, lumber. One man awkwardly carried a truck tire, another a sheet of plywood. Babies peered out, doll-like, from backpacks, while children were gathered up and unwillingly held by the hand as they walked the gangplank to shore.

Compared to Cliff and Long Islands, Peaks was a veritable metropolis. Jones Landing, a bar and restaurant, and Covey Johnson's lobster shack anchored the waterfront. Up the steep hill from the ferry landing was Lisa's Café and Ashmore Realty. Turning left at the top of the hill was Down Front, a seasonal ice cream shop, followed by the Gem art gallery, the US post office, Feeney's Market, and the Cockeyed Gull Restaurant. Next to the Gull was Plante's Marina and Laundromat, a family business with interests in home fuel, excavation, barge service, and a gasoline pump for island cars. Diagonally across from Plante's was the public-safety building, housing the volunteer fire department, a one-room library, and several beds on the second floor for our two policemen. A few doors down was Brad's bike shop, where visitors rented second-hand bikes to pedal the island.

Watching my potential patients climb the hill, I was reminded that this was not a gentrified island. From my recent review of the US census, I knew that Peaks Island was Portland's poorest neighborhood. There might be a hundred or more commuters to Portland each morning, but there was also poverty, particularly inland, where uninsulated shacks were heated by coal and woodstoves.

And from my meetings with the police department I knew there was a darker side to the island: child neglect, alcohol and drug abuse, domestic violence. As I'd observed the Freaks Island sign, another name for Peaks had come to mind—one that I'd heard from various Portland city agencies: Welfare Island.

We walked our bicycles to the top of the hill where we met Sandi's coworker Ellen and purchased ice cream cones. Ellen glanced at her watch. "We have two hours before the next ferry. If you miss that ferry, it'll be another two hours, so we need to move along. We can bike the perimeter of Peaks—it's about four miles—in about twenty-five minutes, so we have plenty of time to stop and talk with folks I've spoken with about designation."

After plunking Kate into the bike seat behind me, we pedaled steadily counterclockwise around the island. It's funny what you notice isn't there when on unfamiliar ground. I noticed that on Peaks there were no stop signs. In fact, there were few signs of any sort: no speed limit or no-parking signs; no warnings to leash your dog or not swim on the beach. Sandi remarked that there were no garages. Ellen said that was because until recently there were only a handful of cars on the island.

We pulled over at Ellen's neighbor's house to talk designation. Halfway through a cup of coffee, Ellen's friend called another neighbor to come and sit with us. All told, we visited six homes that day—and missed two ferries. Everyone agreed to write detailed letters describing the hardships they experienced, not only with emergencies but for routine health visits. It was impressive. And in the ensuing weeks and months, the ripple effect grew, as I received copies of dozens of letters supporting federal designation.

A month later I boarded the 5:35 evening ferry to Peaks while Sandi visited her mom and dad in New Hampshire. I sat down at the bar at Jones Landing, just off the main wharf, and sipped on a beer, enjoying a spectacular sunset. Abruptly, an anchored sailboat exploded into flames. The fire engulfed the mast and furled sails before spreading fore and aft along the deck. I looked to my left and to my right: It was a tough crowd. No one seemed particularly concerned about the boat except to note that the owner wasn't on board and that he was an idiot.

Chebeague Island was my last meeting. The federal application was finished and ready to go. Of course, it wouldn't hurt to have a few more letters. I was optimistic that the hard work I'd put into designation was paying off. I'd learned enough to avoid some of the pitfalls of my previous island interactions: When on Chebeague, speak Chebeague.

Chebeague is the largest island in Casco Bay. While Cliff, Long, and Peaks are officially Portland city islands, Chebeague is an extension of the township of Cumberland. This shifts the grievances of the island away from Portland to Cumberland. There is a thriving lobster fishery and boat-building tradition on the island but also the unmistakable presence of old money. While a perimeter road hugs the shoreline of Peaks, well-maintained private roads angle off the main road to waterfront property on Chebeague. You can drive for miles on Chebeague and never see the ocean.

People on the island tend to be joiners. There is a historical society and an island council, a library and a community center. One woman I met, Donna Damon, was out seven consecutive nights for different meetings. Not bad for an island of 341 year-round residents.

The quickest way to reach Chebeague is to drive ten miles up the coast from Portland and board a ferry for the ten-minute ride to Stone Wharf. The second ferry landing on Chebeague is at the opposite end of the island. Here the *Island Romance*, on the longer-down-the-bay loop from Portland, drops off and picks up passengers at Chandler Cove. The organizers of our meeting that night had arranged for state officials to get to Chebeague by the longer route—to emphasize the hardship islanders endure for routine and emergency care. Very crafty.

Inside, the meeting hall was packed. Blanchard Bates gave a brief overview of the health-care challenges on Chebeague Island, and several islanders vented their frustrations. "Door-to-door, it's a five- or six-hour trip, what with getting to the Chebeague landing, the ferry ride to town, driving to the doctor, and sitting for the appointment, then timing the next ferry home." Another said, "That's why so many of our health issues become emergencies; it's too difficult to get routine care."

I glanced to my right. The state officials were bobbing their heads in agreement. A good sign.

And then it was my turn to speak. I kept it brief and to the point: I was committed to staffing a clinic two mornings a week on Chebeague

Island. I applauded the work of the volunteer ambulance crew on the island and looked forward to working with them.

A hand shot up. A man asked, "If I get sick, that doesn't mean I have to go to your hospital now, does it?"

"No," I said slowly, not quite clear where this was headed. "If you need to be hospitalized, you can be admitted wherever you wish, the Osteopathic Hospital of Maine—where I'm completing my training in internal medicine—Mercy Hospital, or Maine Medical Center."

"That's what I need to know. If I had a bone problem, maybe the Osteopathic would be okay, but my doctor's not an osteopath, and I need someone who can take care of me if I have a serious problem."

"Certainly. Anyone I take care of out here can go wherever they're most comfortable if they require admission to the hospital. Some of you may use me as a primary care doctor, while others may want to use the clinic when they're sick and can't get into town to see their own doctor."

"Will you be on staff at Mercy or Maine Medical Center?"

"No—their bylaws exclude osteopathic physicians from being on staff just as the Osteopathic Hospital doesn't allow MDs on staff."

"That's what I thought."

I stood there, hands in pockets, as a number of muffled side conversations spread through the crowd. I leaned forward into the microphone. "Perhaps this is a good time for me to explain exactly what an osteopathic physician is." The murmuring quieted down. I realized tonight's meeting was as much about my DO background as it was about learning about federal health-care designation.

"First, MDs and DOs are licensed to do the same things—practice medicine in its entirety. Some DOs are family doctors, while others choose to specialize in surgery, obstetrics, cardiology, rheumatology, gastroenterology—you name it. But if we're licensed to do the same work, how are DOs different?

"The answer goes back to the 1870s, when Andrew Still, a medical doctor, grew dissatisfied with the medical practices of the time. Remember, this was when leeches were in use for bloodletting and surgery was performed without anesthesia. Heavy metals such as arsenic and mercury were still commonly prescribed to combat disease. Dr. Still was attracted to the concept that a healthy mind and well-functioning musculoskeletal system were important to the general health of an individual. Now, he didn't abandon all medical treatments or surgery; he simply blended the art of osteopathic manipulation and nutritional advice with the successful medical treatments of the day.

"His ideas were not well accepted, and eventually he made a complete break from the MD community and founded the first osteopathic medical school in Des Moines, Iowa, in 1879. Others soon followed, and today there are nineteen DO medical schools in the United States. But it was never easy. Osteopathic practice in some states was limited to manipulation alone. DOs were denied hospital privileges even in states where they had full practice rights. And so they formed their own medical societies, built their own hospitals, developed their own training programs, and gradually built up enough political power to overturn the limited practice laws.

"Even though many hospitals around the country are mixed staff, MDs and DOs practicing side by side, in Maine a separate but equal status exists. So here I am, standing before you, a graduate of the Kansas City University of Medicine and Bioscience, which I attended for four years after graduating from Bates College. After medical school, I performed a year of internship followed by a three-year internal medicine residency at the Osteopathic Hospital of Maine."

The same man was standing, waiting to be recognized. "Yes?" I asked.

"So, this whole deal is wide open then? I mean, say we go along with this federal designation business and qualify as a designated whatever."

"A health manpower–shortage area," I interjected.

"You'd be in the running, but we could pick who we want from the pool, is that right?"

Sophie Glidden, the federal program's state representative who'd worked closely with me for the past six months, rose from her seat and grudgingly agreed. "Yes, technically that's true. We've been working closely on this project with Doctor Radis, but in the end the rules are clear: the designated area chooses the physician from those in a nationwide pool who have a public-health scholarship payback."

I found myself slumping into my chair, wishing I could quietly disappear out the back door. What in the world had I been thinking?

Albion Miller, the oldest fisherman on the island, rose on spindly legs and slowly looked the crowd over. In his younger years, Albion had handlined cod, alone, in winter, in his double-ended dory on the outer reaches of the bay. I had helped take care of him the year prior when he had been admitted to the Osteopathic Hospital of Maine with a hand infection requiring surgery and IV antibiotics. He was exactly the kind of person I'd hoped to treat on Chebeague Island.

"Look around," he said to the assembly. "I don't see none of those other possible applicants here tonight. I see this young fella, Doctor Radis, sitting here getting grilled like he's tryin' to sell us a bill of goods. Some of you may remember my infection a few years back. Came off Chebeague in bad shape and was admitted to the Osteopathic Hospital. Take a look at me now: I'm fit as a fiddle." With that, Albion twirled around for all to see. "Now, I know for a fact that he's been out to Cliff and Long Island—even tried to be polite to them people on Peaks Island. I say we give this young man the support he deserves."

That, as it turned out, was the turning point.

There were other applicants interested; an island practice has a certain mystical attraction that an inner-city practice does not. But these were the Reagan years, and the National Health Service Corps budget had been slashed. The year the Casco Bay islands was finally designated a health manpower–shortage area, the feds created a new category for scholarship recipients: the private-practice option. Only there was no "option." There would be no federal financial support for newly designated sites. I'd be on my own.

Almost overnight, the applicant pool dried up. My residency director, Dr. Phil Slocum, had it right: if it were possible to make a living on the islands, surely someone would have been doing it by now. Confirming this view, Bruce Kenney, the part-time physician staffing the Peaks Island Health Center, gave notice that he was leaving to concentrate on his in-town practice.

In the end, I was the only applicant.

I accepted the position.

My plan was to staff the Peaks Island Health Center three days and one evening a week, drive up the coast to the Chebeague Island ferry two afternoons a week, and be available for house calls on Cliff and

Long Island. Oh—and admit and manage my patients at the Osteo-pathic Hospital of Maine.

I was too naive, too stubborn, too confident that I could meet any challenge to admit that perhaps I was in over my head. But I surely was.

CHAPTER THREE

**There are really only two kinds of weather here—two that
matter, anyway.**
1. You can leave.
2. You can't leave.
                    —Eva Murray, *The Working Waterfront* *

B
ud Perry was a no-show for his follow-up appointment. I
knocked on his apartment door on my way home from evening
hours at the health center. No answer. I knocked a second time.
It's not pleasant visiting a possibly dead person.

"The door's unlocked! Beer's in the refrigerator!"

In the living room, Bud sat in his recliner, smoking a pipe, sipping
a beer, watching television. On the adjacent side table were a collection
of pipes and several pouches of tobacco. On the carpet was a clump of
tobacco. My eyes tracked to the ceiling where smoke curled upward,
smudging the white paint with a muddy brown halo.

"Good evening, Mister . . . Bud. You missed your appointment."

"Wanted to give the pills a day or two to work. What do you
think?"

I switched on the overhead light. "What's on the TV?"

"Hurricane. Big one. It's off the Carolina coast, and the track is
predicted to cross Cape Cod and hit Maine in a few days. Not that
those jokers know anything; these storms always peter out before they
hit New England. Gulf of Maine water is too cold."

---

*Eva Murray, "The Alcatraz of the Willing," *The Working Waterfront*, July 3, 2013,
http://www.workingwaterfrontarchives.org/2013/07/03/the-alcatraz-of-the-willing/.

I clicked on my penlight and assessed the eye with my free hand. The infection had spread. The eyelid was grossly swollen, the conjunctiva around the iris a swollen pale pink. I pressed firmly on the cheek to assess if the infection had localized into an abscess.

Bud reached up and squeezed my forearm, hard. "The light hurts my eye."

I clicked off the penlight.

"Been thinking of going to the hospital." Bud took a draw from his pipe and exhaled slowly. "The Osteopathic. Lisa from the coffee shop is coming by in her truck in a few minutes, and we can take the last car ferry to town. You can get me on the high-tech stuff. Maybe that'll work."

"Good. I'll make the arrangements," I said, thinking that it might be too late to salvage the eye. "I'll call the ER so they can start antibiotics before they take you upstairs. The intern will get you settled in tonight. Is this your med list?" I asked, getting up and retrieving an index card taped to the refrigerator.

"Yeah, yeah."

"You're making the right decision. I'm usually at the hospital by seven a.m." I glanced at the TV. The predicted storm track was dead-on for Casco Bay.

At the hospital the next morning, the eye was no worse. Bud was subdued, his breakfast untouched. The blood cultures I'd drawn at the health center a few days prior were sterile. At least he wasn't septic. Cardiology ordered an echocardiogram of the heart to assess the integrity of the aortic valve, which had been replaced several years ago. Ophthalmology consulted and suggested a change in Bud's glaucoma drops. It turned out that the infection was only the latest insult to his eye. Buried in their note was the comment, *If pain from uncontrolled glaucoma becomes refractory to current medical management, enucleation may be a consideration.* I silently mouthed the word *e-nuc-le-ation*, a word that perfectly embodies the action: to pluck out an eye. Not a particularly pleasant image.

Last evening's blood work was abysmal. The kidney numbers were particularly worrisome. There were two possibilities: Bud was dehydrated, or, more ominously, he was in early kidney failure associated with his infection. I adjusted the rate of intravenous fluids and ordered an ultrasound of the kidneys and repeat lab for the afternoon. As an afterthought, I wrote for a nephrology-service consultation. Dialysis? It certainly wasn't indicated currently, but it would be best to get nephrology on board to fine-tune his care if the kidneys didn't turn around.

After rounding with the medical student and internal medicine resident, I continued up the coast for the ferry to Chebeague Island for clinic hours.

The twenty-minute drive to the Chebeague Island ferry on Cousins Island (a bridged island connected to the mainland) gave me time to organize my thoughts: I glanced at my pocket calendar: *9:00 a.m. ferry to Stone Pier on Chebeague, drive borrowed green Ford truck to clinic, see patients—? house call, 1:30 ferry return to Cousins Island, make 2:15 ferry to Peaks for evening clinic hours.*

As I drove up the coast, I sipped on a cup of Dunkin' Donuts hazelnut coffee and nibbled on a glazed donut. My backpack held a container of juice and a bag of pretzels. I felt supremely organized. Abruptly, my mind flashed back to the Dunkin' Donuts parking lot: Coming out of the store, in one hand I'd held my wallet, juice, and pretzels, in the other hand my coffee. Coming to the car, I had tried to fish my keys out of my front pocket but, failing at this, put the juice and pretzels under an armpit, and . . . laid the wallet on the roof of the car above the driver's door. Shoot!

Hoping against hope, I slid a hand down from the steering wheel and felt for my wallet in my back pocket. Damn! Braking the car, I pulled over on the shoulder and slumped against the steering wheel. I turned the ignition off, opened the door, and hopelessly glanced at the roof. No wallet. Did I have time to turn around and retrace my steps? No. I'd miss the ferry. The next ferry would leave in an hour and a half. For no particular reason, I slowly walked around the car.

There, nestled in the back bumper, was my wallet. *Yes.* Lucky me.

Pulling into the parking lot for the ferry with only minutes to spare, Leon, the parking lot attendant, was cruising the far end of the lot, inspecting cars for stickers. I abruptly turned in to a grassy spot beneath an apple tree. Gathering my backpack and black bag, I gingerly closed the door and surreptitiously cut down the pathway toward the dock.

"Young man, can I help you?"

"Hi! Remember me?" I shouted back.

"Should I? Got a sticker for that car?"

The *Chebeaguer* threw her gears into reverse and lined up the approach to the wharf. From past experience, I knew this was a touch-and-go operation: throw out a gangplank, board the passengers, push off. In three minutes I needed to be on that boat or would twidde my thumbs awaiting the next ferry.

"Clinic day? Doctor Radis?" I dangled my black bag and green satchel in the air.

Leon looked at me vacantly. "Now, listen here, young fella. I don't care if—"

"Thanks!" I yelled as I scurried to the ferry. "The Chebeague council is working on a sticker!"

It was what Mainers call a "finest kind" of day. The bay was flat and reflective, sprinkled with dozens of lobster buoys. Herring and black-backed gulls wheeled overhead. A broad-beamed lobster boat, the *Miss Dotty*, idled by a green navigational can. After pulling a tricolored buoy, the captain attached the thwarp to a hydraulic wheel, and, one by one, a string of five connected wire, rectangular traps emerged from the water. The sternman methodically pawed through the catch on a flat table overhanging the rail: Rock crabs, sea urchins, whelks, seaweed, sculpin, and undersized lobster went flying overboard in all directions. Flipping over a legal-sized lobster, the sternman identified an illegal egg-bearing female, notched the tail, and tossed her overside as well.

There was a seamless economy to the work. The captain positioned the boat, the sternman (or, not uncommonly, sternwoman) banded the claws of legal lobster and dumped them into a holding barrel, the traps were rebated, the string of traps was reset. Repeat for nine hundred traps.

Lobstering is a sustainable fishery because there is virtually no bycatch. Legal-sized lobsters are harvested; nonlegal lobsters are released unharmed. The brass tool all lobstermen carry not only has a minimum-size notch on one edge but a second measure to identify lobster *above* the legal limit. Jumbo lobsters, known as "super breeders," are home free. And lobsters grow their entire life span. The entire operation is curiously low-tech, an anomaly in a world that demands ever-higher productivity.

Poking my head into the wheelhouse of the *Chebeaguer*, I asked Captain Donny why innovations like larger traps or smaller escape vents or high-tech equipment were prohibited, and he said, "Because we'd catch all the lobsters."

Off-loading at the Stone Wharf, I walked over to a huddle of men leaning into the open hood of an ancient green Ford half-ton pickup, the truck a generous island loan for me to use when I visited the island. Albion Miller, the fisherman who'd stood up for me at the Chebeague meeting last spring, explained that they were listening.

"We was in the market finishing our coffee, wondering if you might make the next ferry, and John here suggested we make sure the truck turned over. Been sitting here a week or more. Wouldn't you know, truck don't start. The battery is in good shape. John thought it might be the distributor. He's 'bout finished cleaning the points." John wiped his hands on a grease rag and gave Albion a thumbs-up.

"Let's give her another try," Albion said. The truck rumbled to life, and Albion smacked a palm smartly on his thigh. "Mind if I catch a ride to the clinic, young fella? I've got an appointment in fifteen minutes. Don't want to be late," he laughed.

As we got underway, the road angled into the interior of the four-mile-long island. On our drive to the clinic, we passed solitary cottages and open fields, stands of white birch and a grove of apple trees.

A few minutes later, we pulled into the driveway of the Chebeague Public Safety building, and Albion transitioned from passenger to patient. Inside the ten-by-ten clinic room, my eye was drawn to the scar on Albion's temple, where I'd removed a basal cell carcinoma. Over the last few months, the scar had thinned down and blended with the crease over his eye. Not bad. Albion claimed that he was a walking billboard for my practice.

As I inflated the blood pressure cuff, I looked over Albion's bony fingers. It was a wonder he could cradle a spoon or pull up a zipper. Each individual joint was enlarged and angulated, giving the fingers an S-shaped appearance. When he flexed the fingers to the palm, a series of creaks and snaps was audible. When he released his fist and extended the fingers, the fourth finger of the right hand stayed stubbornly down. Albion waited until I unwrapped the blood pressure cuff before he grabbed the offending finger with the other hand and snapped it open.

I continued to stare at his hands as he struggled to get a set of keys out his pocket. "Bother you much?" I asked.

"By jiminy, you was reading my mind!" Albion smacked his thigh. "That's the exact reason I set up this appointment! Tylenol is just about worthless. Thought you might have a pill to take the ache out of these old fingers."

"I can do that . . . and I think I can fix that fourth finger that doesn't move well. You have what's called a trigger finger. There's a bump on the tendon that catches and prevents you from straightening it out. I could inject the sheath around the tendon with a few drops of cortisone. It might free it up."

"You're the doctor." While I drew up the medication into a syringe, Albion commented on how nice the clinic room looked, what with the new window curtains, and asked who'd donated the painting of the weathered skiffs. Although the space was tight, I had to admit the extra touches brought in by islanders in recent months had created a homey, intimate atmosphere.

The human hand is richly innervated with hundreds of sensory nerve endings, and for most patients anesthetizing a finger is akin to plunging the digit into a hive of angry honeybees. Albion's hand stiffened slightly as the needle penetrated his palm, but he showed no emotion. I injected a steady stream of lidocaine into the sheath of the flexor tendon. Albion took to whistling a mournful tune.

Once the needle was in proper position and the tendon sheath anesthetized, I removed the syringe with a Kelly clamp, and exchanged it with a cortisone-filled syringe before slowly injecting the cortisone along the flexor tendon. Needle out, Band-Aid on, Albion flexed his fingers and lit up a smile.

"By Jesus, those fingers are moving like they belong to a much younger man. Now here's something might come in handy this winter. Knit it myself." Albion pulled out a green, white, and red scarf from his canvas tote bag and laid it out on the table. I'd heard that fishermen often knit in their spare time. It was a solid piece of work. "Sometimes I knit ties, potholders, mittens—you name it."

I thanked him and wrapped the scarf around my neck.

Luckily, Albion was on Medicare, and I could bring his bill back to the Peaks clinic where Kathryn could submit it. Other times it was up to me to muster up my best, "That will be thirty-five dollars." Frankly, I felt sheepish whenever I ask a patient for my fee. Doctors are usually insulated from the money end; we check a box on the bill and hand it to the patient, who pays or delays at the checkout counter. As yet, I hadn't had to dicker with the price of an office visit or procedure, which led me to suspect my rates were on the low side. An occasional patient had gratefully topped off my bill with a pound of fresh scallops or a brace of lobsters.

In all, there were five Chebeague clinic visits that morning: a painful shoulder; a perplexing, painful rash on the left chest—which I fortunately realized was shingles; a four-year-old with a sore throat and ear pain; a lobsterman with a bad back; a carpenter with a painful elbow. A few modern tests were at my disposal. Swabbing the four-year-old's throat, I verified a strep throat by mixing the swab in a solution and adding a drop of reagent. When the fluid turned blue, strep was confirmed rather than a viral illness. The glucometer in my black bag had been indispensable for diagnosing and following diabetes. An inexpensive hemoglobinometer could assess for anemia. For the rest of my diagnostics, I drew blood, labeled the tubes, centrifuged down the samples, and dropped them off at the hospital for processing.

My last patient before the return ferry was a house call. Merle was a large, homebound woman who'd kept meticulous records of her blood sugars and blood pressure. Though her record keeping was superb, the numbers were dismal.

We problem-solved through the out-of-control blood sugars. Merle changed the subject as she surreptitiously dropped a handkerchief over a Milky Way candy bar. From previous visits, I knew that Merle's day was usually spent sitting in her recliner looking outside or watching TV. I suggested that she get outside and walk up and down the driveway at least once a day. She said that she'd try but that her knee kept her from walking more than a few feet. I shifted my attention to the knee. It had a small amount of fluid and creaked as I attempted to assess range of motion. Maybe a cortisone injection could make the knee more comfortable, I thought. If the knee were better, she might walk more. More walking might decrease her appetite and improve her blood pressure and sugars. She readily agreed to the injection.

The distance between Merle's skin and the cavity of her knee joint was twice the distance of a usual knee. I inserted the needle and probed deeper and deeper, injecting a whiff of lidocaine to anesthetize the soft tissues. Merle didn't look up from her romance novel. I frowned; I was as far as I could go. I leaned into the syringe, and I felt the needle enter the joint space. Then, cortisone in, needle and syringe pulled, Band-Aid applied, Merle indicated with a wave of her hand that I gave a "good shot."

I added a note to my pocket calendar: *Bring extra-long spinal needle to Cheb nxt wk; keep on-site.* Based on Merle's meticulously recorded blood sugars, I adjusted her oral diabetic medication and added fifty milligrams to her background dose of Lopressor for better control of her hypertension. Before leaving, I unwrapped an Ace bandage to evaluate the chronic nonhealing ulcer on the outer aspect of her ankle and redressed it with Silvadene. She could be better. She could be worse.

Back on the mainland, I dropped by the Osteopathic Hospital on my way to the ferry and was reassured by the cardiology note that Bud Perry's aortic valve replacement was free of infection and functioning well. Dr. Miller, in ophthalmology, remained concerned that Bud's glaucoma readings remained elevated. Now that he was using the drops under supervision, the pressures were slowly falling; no surprise there, but Dr. Miller wanted to max out a combination of two medications before considering other options.

Bud's kidney function showed slight improvement from the previous night, but an ultrasound demonstrated that both kidneys were atrophic—undersized and permanently damaged due to the effects of chronic uncontrolled hypertension. I scribbled a note in my pocket calendar: *Remove ibuprofen from Bud's apartment, toxic to kidneys!!*

Bud was more animated and disagreeable, which I took as a good sign. The facial cellulitis was perhaps a smidgen better. He wouldn't require surgery. There was nothing to drain.

I caught the 2:15 ferry back to Peaks and bicycled home for a quick dinner. In the living room I played nearly three-year-old Kate's favorite game: With a running start she jumped—or, more accurately, flew—off the bottom stair, landing into my arms. Repeat. Sandi looked exhausted. She was working three days a week in Portland at the therapeutic nursery, which meant dropping Kate off at Tina's daycare up the hill before the 8:15 ferry and picking her up off the 4:30 ferry from town. Even with my best efforts, I was rarely home before six or seven. Sandi was doing 80 percent of the cleaning, 90 percent of the parenting, and 100 percent of the grocery shopping and bill paying. I vacuumed, regularly changed Kate's diapers, and cleaned an occasional bathroom—in the big scheme, not enough to put much of a dent in our household responsibilities.

I felt guilty heading out again, but an evening clinic was the only chance for well-off commuters to be seen at the health center. The painful reality was that many of my regular patients lacked insurance and were not paying their bills or copays. Despite Kathryn's education efforts, many didn't seem to understand that although I was a National Health Service Corps physician, there was no federal support for the clinic. Maybe, I thought, a sign at the front desk would help.

Evening clinic hours were light. A high school teacher and an insurance agent came in with productive coughs associated with yellow-green sputum and fever. At the bases of both their right lungs were prominent crackles, a strange coincidence: the diagnosis, community-acquired pneumonia. Neither could bring up a sputum sample for me to culture. I began them both on antibiotic samples and penned in a follow-up for one week later.

A carload of elderly nuns from Saint Michael's retirement convent on the island arrived together. Their active health problems listed on the inside page of their charts rivaled Bud Perry's. The nuns, without a doubt, were already my favorite patients. Sister Marie Henry blessed the prescription bottles. Sister Judy dutifully wrote down every word of my instructions as if what I said were gospel. If I suggested they walk, I'd find Sister Janice on the backshore with several sisters in tow.

Then there was Sister Mia. I knew that I was in for it when I shook her hand at our first visit and she corrected me: "Call me Sarge," her nickname from teaching parochial school. "And if you were thinking I didn't brook no nonsense from the students, you would have it correct." Crossing her plump arms, she stared me down. I squirmed uneasily, and she roared with laughter.

Today Sarge was in for a routine checkup. I breezed into the room and scanned her chart, as the blood pressure, circled in red by Kathryn, finally registered: 232 over 120.

"Jesus!" The Lord's name squeaked out in protest.

Sarge affixed me with her best I'm-coming-across-the-aisle-to-rap-your-knuckles scowl.

"I mean, *jeepers*—your blood pressure is too high," I said.

"I'm uncomfortable," she said. "It's the chair."

Now that I noticed, Sarge was wedged into the exam chair, her brown habit stretched tightly across her waist. The room was not overly warm, but a glistening of sweat pooled at the edge of her white hair. Reaching up, she smoothed back a stray swath of hair and padded her hands dry with a paper towel.

In these cases, I knew the best strategy was to move on and not overly focus on the abnormal blood pressure. I'd take it again in a few minutes; perhaps it had been taken in error. I reached out and palpated the front of Sister Mia's neck.

"My . . . my goodness!" I gasped.

"Doctors have told me that my thyroid is enlarged. Do you find it so today?"

The thyroid was enormous. It was the size of a lemon. There was a solid nodule on the left lobe. It felt cancerous. I moved on to examining her feet. That should be safe enough. I palpated for the two distal blood vessels—dorsalis pedis and tibialis posterior. "Little bit of swelling down here," I noted. "Are you watching your salt intake?" With her excess abdominal fat she couldn't see me but could feel me palpate first the right foot, then the left. I went back to the right. No pulse. Left, no pulse.

What in God's name are you doing down there?"

"I'm checking your pulses."

"And how might you find them?"

"They're less than I expected."

"So, is that good or bad?"

I weighed my words carefully. "We need blood to reach our feet. When we have less reaching the feet than we should, we—rather, *you* are at risk for claudication or—"

"Gangrene. Go ahead and say it. I could lose my feet. Goodness gracious, by the power of Mary!" She grabbed a loose magazine and fanned herself. Now she was really sweating.

"So," I said, sitting down, aware this keg might blow at any moment. Wasn't there an organ system I could examine on this woman that was functioning as God intended? "So, how long have you been retired on the island?" I was determined to say or do something benign.

"Three years. We assist Father Flanigan with Mass at Saint Christopher. We are never fully retired; the Lord's work is never done."

"I see. That's so true." I knew she was waiting for me, daring me, to take her blood pressure again.

Suddenly she grinned. "Doctor Radis, your wife, Dusty—I've seen her walking with your daughter up to the playground."

"Dusty?" I blinked. "Sandi?"

"Sandi? Your daughter's name is Sandi? We understood it to be Kate."

It's my turn to smile. "Sandi is my wife. Her hair is blonde, and at the end of the day"—I lowered my voice—"coming in off the trail, she can look a little dusty. And, yes, Kate's name is Kate." Sister Mia punched me heavily in the arm, shaking with laughter.

As we chatted, she extended her arm, and I inflated the cuff. The manometer needle drifted past 240 without a whisper, and I exhaled: 220, 200, 190 . . . finally at 178, a steady drb-drb-drb pulsed with her heartbeat. 178 over 94. Better. At least I wouldn't need to call the rescue fireboat; an adjustment in her medications might be all that was necessary.

"Sister Mia, you have labile hypertension. It can shoot up, it would seem, at the slightest provocation. Cut down on your salt, join Sister Marie Henry on her morning walks, and the fluid pill—the HCTZ— double it to fifty milligrams daily. Also, the Catapres—the orange pill? I want you to double it to point-two milligrams twice daily. That should block some of the sharp peaks that raise your risk of a stroke."

She checked in her purse for how many Catapress and HCTZ remained in her prescription bottle and whether there were refills. Satisfied, she waved for me to proceed

"We'll need to check your kidney function and blood counts today, and I want you to go uptown tomorrow for a test, an ultrasound of your neck. I feel it's very—"

"Okay. That will be fine."

"While you're there, we'll scan your thyroid and check the circulation in the lower legs as well."

"Of course."

She would go. I was stunned. No fussing, grumping, confounding, or deal making. On a roll, I added, "And one thing more—your weight. What can we do about your weight?" I sensed an involuntary stiffening. Oops, careful. Danger! Danger! I would either be rapped across the knuckles or witness a cerebral hemorrhage.

Outside, a horn blew. The sisters in their minivan waved in unison when they saw me peeking out the blinds. I waved back, noting that Sister Marie Henry had crushed the plastic recycling container with the front wheel. Here's a paradox: These icons of religiosity were rumored to lack a legitimate driver's license between them. It wasn't surprising; Peaks Island cars required neither registration nor an inspection sticker, so why bother with the technicalities of a license?

On my way home I dropped by Feeney's Market. Milk, eggs, candles, batteries, bottled water, and beer were already sold out. Outside the Gull, islanders discussed pulling their boats if predictions held and Maine was in for a direct hit.

The next morning, a Saturday, the sound of hammering began at dawn. Sheets of plywood were nailed over exposed windows and screen doors. A line of pickup trucks with trailers waited their turn at the Centennial Beach boat ramp. I learned that Casco Bay Lines would suspend ferry service if sustained winds were greater than forty knots.

Big John, our gentle six-foot-eight policeman, called me at home and requested that I remain on the island through the hurricane. If there were injuries, he noted, it might be impossible to transfer islanders to the mainland for a few days. I brought my emergency kit tackle box home and reviewed my what-ifs.

Unlike North Carolina, where the barrier islands barely rise above sea level, Peaks and the other islands in Casco Bay are the tops of flooded ridges and mountaintops. Though we were only thirty yards from the beach, our rental house was a good twenty-five feet above high tide. Flooding shouldn't be an issue. What's more, we were on the lee side of the island, safe from wind-driven surf from the open ocean. I was confident our location was safe but less sure about the windows and roof of our house. Sandi rummaged down in the basement and located a hammer and two sheets of plywood. Together we nailed the plywood over the two most exposed windows. That evening, I checked the batteries in our flashlights and placed a candle with a book of matches in each room. We waited. Sandi called me over to the TV.

"Chuck, there is a story on Peaks Island on Channel 8."

We sat together on the floor, Kate nestled on my lap, and leaned against the couch. "Brenda, we're here tonight at the Casco Bay Lines," the newscaster began. "With Hurricane Gloria bearing down on Maine, Portland has recommended evacuation of the city islands. Local schools in downtown Portland have been designated by the Red Cross as emergency shelters, and we'll be interviewing residents from Peaks Island coming off the boat presently."

We munched on popcorn as the camera focused on two crewmen wrestling the gangplank over the side of the *Machigonne* as it docked in Portland. The camera panned the deck, then down the gangplank. Not a single person off-loaded. Instead, the camera panned the long line of islanders waiting to board the ferry *to* Peaks. The line snaked around the corner of the freight terminal. Carts were piled high with sheets of plastic, two-by-fours, lanterns, bedding and tools, and, oddly, suitcases, and fishing poles. A sober-faced man wearing a Hawaiian shirt and lugging an immense potted plant was asked by the reporter, "What in the world are you thinking, heading out to Peaks Island when city officials have recommended evacuation?

"Hurricane party."

Later that evening I checked in with the police, assuring them I had emergency supplies at home. "I'll sit tight here tomorrow unless you

need me. I heard that, because no one is leaving the island, they've
designated the school as an emergency shelter. Are you running out of
cots in the gym?"

"So far," John admitted, "nobody has shown up at the school. The
gym is empty. Crazy, if you ask me, with all these flimsy cottages."

Before bedtime, Sandi and I walked the beach. A steady, light driz-
zle fell. The wind was kicking up whitecaps across the channel closer to
Little Diamond Island. I shone my flashlight into the water at a raft of
seabirds—eiders, buffleheads, and black ducks hugging the shore.

By daybreak bands of heavy rain fell. The police called and
informed me that Casco Bay Lines was suspending service after the next
boat. I made one last run to the grocery store and watched the ferry to
Peaks plow through wave after wave of rolling green water. I was about
to turn away when I spied a solitary sail, a windsurfer, shadowing the
ferry just shy of House Island. Coming up on the bow, he waved to the
crew before launching skyward off the crest of the wave.

Little Ricky Hogan jogged past, leaning into the wind. "Doctor
Radis, did you hear? I made the cross-country team, and our first meet
is next week! Look, I have new sneakers!"

I waved back and grinned. Ricky cut up Luther Street and down a
dirt path to his house. Crazy kid. Driving home, my truck was rocked by
the wind, and as I passed by the school, a huge limb came crashing down
onto the playground. I realized our backup plan might be faulty. If the
storm was strong enough to take down a tree, electrical lines might be
down as well. Parking the truck, I made a mad dash for the door.

For the next six hours, we huddled in the living room, the fireplace
to our backs, fearful of broken glass. Sandi arranged a nest of blankets
and pillows for Kate, and we entertained ourselves by playing hide-and-
seek beneath the covers and reading picture books. The porch windows
on the south side bowed and rattled in the swirling wind.

Outside, the rain fell in thick, horizontal sheets. First Portland, then
Casco Bay, then the beach disappeared in a swirl of driven spray and
sand. At noon, the radio informed us that the storm track had veered
westward over Massachusetts and southern New Hampshire. Even so,
the local news reported sustained winds of eighty-five miles per hour in
Portland. I couldn't imagine what 110 must feel like. Encouraged by the

revision, I peeped out our front door window only to see our neighbor's massive oak suddenly uproot and splay across the road, dragging a telephone pole and strings of wire to the ground.

That, as it turned out, was Gloria's best shot. Hour by hour, the stormed weakened, until by midafternoon Gloria was officially downsized to a tropical storm. Half the state of Maine was without power. Remarkably, we still had electricity. Kate took a nap.

"Looks like the storm is breaking up," I remarked to Sandi.

"We made it, didn't we?" she smiled nervously. "We're not in the eye or something like that, are we?"

"No, the radio says it's veered inland." I opened the back door. To the west, scattered clouds raced across the sky. There was the pungent smell of salty air. The sun peeked through, casting an incandescent light on the point of Little Diamond Island. "Looks like high tide," I said innocently. "I'll bet the backshore of Peaks is wild. I wonder if surf is coming across the road."

"Chuck Radis, we are not driving to the backshore, if that's what you're thinking," Sandi's eyes flared. "Look at that tree up there by the road. Wires are down; we couldn't get to the backshore even if we wanted to."

"Of course. You're right."

"Chuck, I am not taking Kate outside and have you drive the truck over live wires. That's stupid."

I nodded. Of course, Sandi was right. I waited another hour. The island was bathed in full sunshine, and the wind backed off to a stiff breeze. "I promise, we won't drive over any wires. If we come to a downed tree or wires, we'll just turn around. Let's at least get outside and walk up to the truck. It'll be dark in another hour." Secretly, I knew that Sandi wanted to see the backshore. By tomorrow, the surf would be down. Kate, awake from her nap, pleaded to go outside. Sandi pulled the curtains back; she was mulling it over, gauging the risk.

"But we turn around if we come to a wire across the road," she announced.

"Absolutely."

Ten minutes later, the three of us were bundled up and driving to the backshore. A downed tree blocked our way on Pleasant Avenue.

I backed up and turned back onto Island Avenue, past Down Front. Debris was everywhere. We crept along and turned up Island Avenue past the Lions Club. Sandi pointed out flattened sheds and roofs needing major repairs. Up Luther Street we spied a boat on a trailer flipped upside down and blown sideways against a car.

Turning away from Down Front toward the backshore, thickets of beach rose and bittersweet were flattened along the roadway amid piles of gravel and larger boulders. Clumps of surf foam blew by, covering the road where it dipped around a low point. We made the last turn to the backshore as a massive wave cracked over shore ledge, sending giant plumes of spray skyward.

But we were not alone. Before us a raucous party was in full swing. Dozens of cars were parked along the backshore. Islanders danced on the road, laughing and screaming at the tops of their lungs. It would seem all of Peaks Island was outside. We spied three teenagers, arms linked, lurching off balance, falling to their knees when the wind suddenly dropped off. Another group played a dangerous game of tag, sprinting down the beach and tagging it before an avalanche of churning ocean water engulfed them.

"Not our children," Sandi said, holding onto Kate's hand tightly. "Not now, not ever."

CHAPTER FOUR

The diseases are easy; the patients are hard.
—Marc Miller, MD

Bud Perry's swollen cheek loomed overhead, lambasting me for giving him poison. Mrs. Tingley sat stoically, ashen blue, her oxygen tube crimped by a monarch butterfly. She asked me why Bud wasn't getting better. I was on the water, balanced on a lobster buoy, when I heard a metallic CUNK and sat up suddenly in bed, awakening Sandi.

I looked around our darkened bedroom, wisps of my Alice in Wonderland dream dissipating like early morning fog. "Did you hear that?" I said, "It sounded like a boat hitting a ledge."

"Chuck," Sandi said, "you're having a dream. You'll wake Kate."

I opened the curtain and peered out at the beach. A full moon hung over the water. Wisps of snow skittered across the beach like tumbleweed. Except for a rowboat flipped upside down above the high-tide mark the beach was deserted. I looked at my watch: 1:30 a.m. Sitting on the bed, I felt Sandi nestle against my back and rearrange the covers, but before lying down, I peeked out the street side window.

"Sandi, there's a van up there."

"That's very interesting. Now come back to bed."

"Wait a minute, there's somebody walking around. Hey, he just fell down in the snow. He's getting up—no, he's down again. Damn." Hurrying downstairs, I pulled on my boots and parka and grabbed my black bag.

As I approached the van, the man was back on his feet, swaying like a lumbering bear that's broken into a jug of whiskey: big-boned, powerful, unpredictable. He emptied his bladder against our mailbox. I asked him if he was okay.

He looked up, head rolling. It was John. "I'm awfully sorry."

Sorry for what? Sorry for being drunk? The front end of his van was crumpled, and both headlights were shattered. Metallic debris and shards of glass lay scattered on the edge of the road. I reached into my pocket for a penlight, thinking, head injury—keep him talking. A Jeep braked to a stop behind the van, and Eric, one of the island policemen, stepped out.

"Doctor Radis, is that you?" He swept his flashlight across the front end of the van. "Oh my." While I examined John, Eric waded through a snowdrift to our maple tree and ran his hand over the trunk. "Funny. Your tree's fine."

It didn't add up. The front end of John's van was crumpled, but then I saw a vague, dark mound across the street. Planted in the ditch, the rear end compressed like an accordion, was our Honda Civic.

John suddenly pulled himself together and correctly answered Officer Eric's questions. He walked a reasonably straight line. Amazingly, there wasn't a bump or scrape on him. Eric told him to get into the Jeep; he'd take him home. Pulling me aside, John apologized again and asked if I'd mind if we kept this off his insurance. We could settle this up tomorrow. Eric kicked the snow off his boots and opened the driver's side of the police Jeep.

Wait. That was it? I was wild-eyed. "No ticket?" I pulled back my hood. "This guy must've been going fifty coming down the hill and totaled my car, and you're not even giving him a ticket?"

For the next fifteen minutes, Officer Eric explained that, because he didn't actually see any reckless driving and John did walk a straight line, and because he didn't have a breathalyzer in the Jeep, and by the time he called for the police boat and got John uptown his alcohol level would be normal, he basically couldn't do anything except drive John home, get him to bed.

I was thinking, it's Officer Eric who wants to get to bed. "John, *you are* going to make good on the car with Doctor Radis, now, aren't you?" he asked. John said he and I had already talked.

I wanted to punch someone.

I took my boots off in the kitchen on yesterday's newspaper, flicked on the electric teapot, and reviewed the week. One thing was for certain: I wasn't making much money. Kathryn was many things, but, unfortunately, top-notch billing clerk wasn't one of them. Office manager wasn't one of my strengths; only last week I'd found tucked into an unlabeled folder next to the patient appointment book the charges I'd submitted to her for a patient I'd admitted to the Osteopathic Hospital late last summer.

The osteopathic angle? For the most part, those who were adamant they'd never see an osteopath bypassed me and went to town. From time to time, an acute illness would drive them into my office on Peaks or Chebeague, and those visits were uncomfortable for both of us. I could feel their distrust. At the conclusion of one visit, a husband who had accompanied his wife into the exam room for her urinary tract symptoms wanted me to call their doctor in Portland to ask him if he thought my choice for an antibiotic was reasonable. Sorry. I wasn't going to do that. Or worse, Kathryn once roomed a patient and was in the process of taking her vitals when she looked up and noticed my diploma and state license on the wall. She took off so fast, the BP cuff was still dangling from her right arm as she hit the front desk.

I sipped on honeyed tea as droplets of water liquefied from the frosty edges of my mustache and pooled on the table. It's not that I was sitting around. I rarely had an opening in my schedule at the Peaks clinic. Several times in the last month I'd left Chebeague on a later afternoon ferry in order to see the last patient. House calls have been steady; on Peaks I averaged three a week, most of them after hours. On Chebeague I have a list of frail elderly patients I see each month in their homes. Visits to Cliff and Long Island keep me busy. It was the commute, the time on the water, that's a killer. That and missed ferries coming back from Portland. I didn't even want to think about how many times I'd parked my car and run for the 5:35 evening ferry from Portland to Peaks only to stand limply by the landing as the *Machigonne* pulled away into the harbor, the next ferry not scheduled to depart until 7:15.

In the margin of my At-a-Glance pocket calendar I totaled up my weekly commute by the Casco Bay ferry—eleven and a half hours—and idly sketched a boat. Drifting, the warm mist of the tea soothing my eyes, I imagined an ideal craft. Not too big—say, eighteen to twenty-two feet, cuddy cab to cut the wind, dependable outboard, maybe a spare . . . what do they call it . . . a kicker, if the main engine were to fail.

"Chuck," Sandi's hand rested on my shoulder. "Let's get some rest. I can't go back to sleep." She brushed a strand of blonde hair out of her face and sat down on the bench, leaning on my shoulder. Spying the boat sketch under my elbow, her voice sharpened. "Let me count the reasons why we shouldn't buy a boat. You don't know anything about boats. We can't afford a boat. It's too dangerous. Wasn't it this week the police wouldn't take you out to Long Island for a house call because the float's been pulled?"

I knew I was up against an immovable mountain of logic. "Lobster boat took me over from Chebeague to Cliff Island. It was easy; no problem."

"And what—he tied up against some rickety ladder while you went off to see his aunt? Chuck, we lose a car"—she looked up the hill— "we buy another car; we lose a boat, and you might be on it."

"Of course, you're right. Makes perfect sense. There's no logic in getting a boat," I said, thinking, not now, not this winter.

Friday morning, turning onto Sterling Street, a raw northeast breeze at my back, I spied Bud Perry pacing at the front door of the Peaks Island Health Center. Draped over his thick frame was a plum polar expedition parka with a tunneled hood, and over his hands enormous gray mittens. With the end of his white walking stick, he reached overhead and rapped the edge of a two-foot stalactite, sending a shower of ice shattering onto the porch. "Some knucklehead should get off their butt and clear this porch before you open for the public."

"Good morning, Bud," I said, unlocking the front door and going about the business of opening the clinic. "You're early. I'll be with you directly." Bud emerged from his coat and settled into a chair before taking out his pipe and lighter.

Kathryn came through the door, grabbed the lighter, and asked Bud how he was on this delightful winter day. In answer, Bud pursed his lips and emitted a low-pitched grumble, like a deflating whoopee cushion. At the scale, more displeasure: 238 pounds.

"I'm wasting away, every visit, two, three pounds. Doc, when you going to figure out why I'm melting away? Measure me." Kathryn raised the bar on the scale and removed Bud's grimy hat. Bud stretched out, unfolding rounded shoulders and tipping his chin upward to reach the bar.

"Six-feet-one," Kathryn lied, quickly sliding the bar down, "still exactly six-feet-one," and led him into an exam room.

Pausing outside the door, I pulled Bud's chart and reviewed his problem list. The facial infection had required a week of intravenous antibiotics late last summer. My god, those last few days in the hospital had been miserable for everyone. Arthritis in the knee, stable, still walking, I noted. The recent letter from his ophthalmologist noted that Bud was legally blind. At least there was no mention of enucleation. I smiled pleasantly at Bud, who leaned, stone-faced, on his cane.

Flipping through the chart, I familiarized myself with his previous visits to the health center. Heart surgery four years ago, aortic valve replaced and two vessels bypassed, came through that like a champ. History of bleeding ulcer, bladder cancer, recurrent prostate infections, peripheral vascular disease, poorly controlled diabetes, renal insufficiency. More dead than alive for a sixty-seven-year-old. Wow—320 pounds when he went in for heart surgery four years ago.

"What can I do for you today, Bud?"

"Can't feel my feet. Dizzy. Keep passing out. Other than that, I feel like crap."

Sitting, his blood pressure was normal, at 116 over 72, but standing was another story: 82 over 66, low enough to account for the dizziness. Kathryn knocked on the door and handed me a lab slip from last Friday's blood draw.

"Bud, your blood counts are low—low enough to cause fatigue, shortness of breath, or even light-headedness. Your kidney numbers are abnormal, but at least they're stable. Anemia often develops when the kidneys are damaged by diabetes or high blood pressure. But it could be your ulcer again. Any change in your bowels? Are they looking black or tarry? How much alcohol are you drinking?"

Bud pulled a Kleenex from his front pocket, cleared his throat, and spat into it. "If you read the chart, I stopped drinking two years ago, and, no, my ulcer ain't acting up."

I unlaced Bud's boots and pulled them off. On the outer edge of his right sock was a dab of crusted blood. Beneath the fifth toe was a shallow ulcer. Flipping through my notes from his admission to the Osteopathic Hospital four months ago there was no mention of lower-extremity ulcers or numbness in the feet.

I frowned as I examined the foot. His Achilles reflex was absent at the heel, and he could barely feel me touching his toes. The diagnosis, peripheral neuropathy, probably related to his uncontrolled diabetes. Oh my, where to start? The dizziness? Toe ulcer? Anemia? Diabetes?

I gathered my thoughts. "An ulcer you can't feel or see can be dangerous. You need to keep a dab of Neosporin on the ulcer and wear only clean white socks. If you can't see the toe, maybe Lisa from the coffee shop can stop by and help you out. Second, cut your blood pressure medication in half. When you stand, your pressure drops by thirty points. That's the reason you feel light-headed. But don't stop the blood pressure medication completely. It was only last month that your blood pressure was way too high. Third, take another half of the blue pill, your diabetes pill, and take it with your evening meal. Your blood sugars are still way too high." I finished writing out the instructions in large print and handed him the piece of paper. "And bend over. I need to do a rectal exam to check for blood. There might be more than one reason your anemia is getting worse."

Bud dropped his pants and bent over. "Put a glove on this time, Doc."

With the tip of my finger I palpated the prostate and reached upward to assess for a possible mass. Except for a small hemorrhoid, the exam was normal. I dabbed a guaiac card with stool from my glove tip and added a drop of solution to the specimen. A blue tinge means blood is present. I stared intently at the fecal specimen, waiting for the telltale blue tinge of blood. None. More than likely, the anemia was secondary to the progressive failure of his kidneys.

The hat went back on first, then the pipe. Pulling himself up by his cane, he made for the door, but not before blurting out a dirty joke about two nuns unexpectedly coming across a priest while he undressed. At the punch line, he tittered an incongruous high-pitched laugh and said, "And the best part, I told that joke to one of the retired nuns up at the convent, and she laughed! Didn't have a clue!"

I skimmed the name on the next chart: Ricky Hogan, and thought, home from school, sick, flu bug, maybe. Cross-country season had been a success. Even as a freshman he was one of the best runners on the team. This winter I'd seen Ricky running through the slush and ice around the island in an effortless, churning stride. Sandi mentioned to me last month that the Boy Scout Troop Ricky had joined on Peaks was going to camp out on the backshore later this winter. She kept track of that kind of news, knowing that without an involved dad Ricky needed structure and a positive environment.

Inside the exam room, Ricky was curled up in a chair, all legs, his arms wrapped lightly around his knees, rocking. He reminded me of a colt, still wet from birth, gangly and bony, unsure if it can stand.

"Doctor Radis, I can hardly swallow. My mom's at work, but she told me to come over."

Inside his mouth, the tonsils nearly kissed up against each other. The lymph nodes in his neck were enlarged. Laying Ricky down, I felt for the spleen in the upper left quadrant of the abdomen. It was tender and enlarged, reaching down a third of the way to the pelvic rim.

I drew blood for a quick Monospot, one of the few on-site diagnostic tests at the health center, and placed a drop onto the test card. It was positive. Epstein-Barr, the virus responsible for mononucleosis, is a common virus in young adults, and antibiotics are ineffective. Thankfully, our own immune system gradually corrals the virus, forcing it into retreat while the body recovers. I showed Ricky the positive test and ran through the usual precautions: Don't share drinking cups or utensils, wash hands, keep up your fluid intake, and call if you develop a high fever (secondary bacterial infections can often follow on the heels of mononucleosis).

"You'll need extra sleep, and, of course no running until—"

"But I've got to run," he interrupted.

"Not while the virus is active. If you have a mild case, you'll be back running before you know it. For now," I repeated, "no running." He nodded sullenly if not convincingly. Patients were backing up in the waiting room; I needed to move on and scribbled a note to his mother and another to excuse him from gym class.

Dawn. Sandi and I bundled up Kate into her snowsuit, and headed off for the 7:15 ferry to buy a battery in town. If we had time, and there surely should be time, we planned on visiting the Children's Museum. True to his word, John had paid me the week before for our Honda Civic he'd totaled. We'd since bought a truck with a battery problem from a neighbor up Luther Street. It worked fine in the afternoon but not in the morning. We had sixteen minutes to walk three quarters of a mile. I alternated holding Kate's hand and carrying her. Sandi strode ahead. Five minutes before, I'd run back to the house for the keys to our in-town car. Marital advice to self: don't make Sandi late.

To the east, a faint sliver of sky lightened the horizon; to the west, a waxing half-moon set over Portland's skyline. We trudged silently up the hill, our boots scuffing fresh powder. Bud Perry sat on the rock wall in front of the Catholic church. From his pipe a wisp of smoke hung like a shroud in the stillness of the coming day. As we passed, Bud suddenly squawked a Donald Duck imitation, startling Kate who grinned back.

Crossing the gangplank of the *Machigonne* with minutes to spare, we settled onto a green slatted wooden bench for the twenty-minute ride to Portland. I told Sandi I was sorry I had almost made us miss the boat. Saying nothing, she pulled out a paperback and opened it, leaning lightly against my parka.

Kate pleaded to walk around. The ride was too brief for the snowsuit to come off, so I stuffed her cap in my pocket and pulled off the drawstring mittens. Freed, she toddled forward like a drunken sailor, weaving and lurching with outstretched arms, steadying herself on the swaying deck.

I joined the toddler crowd at their favorite pole in time to see Kate collide with a boy. They both fell, but neither cried. I apologized to the mother, who shrugged and said, "One of these days they'll learn." Okay, done the pole. What's over there? She spied a bright yellow package beneath a bench and wandered over to investigate, bumping into knees and boots and coats. People patted her on the head as she passed by like an errant puppy.

My beeper vibrated. I was on call. It was the emergency room at the Osteopathic. I made a phone signal to Sandi and pointed upstairs. She closed her book and patted the bench for Kate to sit down.

Up top, the bow of the *Machigonne* plowed into a steady twenty-knot breeze. We'd passed the lee of Little Diamond Island, and slabs of blue-gray water pounded against the bow, sending a fountain of spray up onto the top deck. Scattered chunks of shimmering pack ice wallowed on the surface. From the pilothouse, Captain Jimmy waved in my direction. Well, it wasn't actually a wave, more a subtle raised eyebrow. I pointed to my beeper and pantomimed a phone call. Last summer, when I'd rambled on about how I was the new doctor on the island and sometimes I get beeped and sometimes it's okay for me to wait until I get to Portland but sometimes I needed to answer my page right away, he'd said "Fine," then turned back to piloting the boat. Today, as I closed the door to the pilothouse, he said, "Phone?"

I dialed the marine operator, who connected me to the hospital. Involuntarily, I stiffened and tapped my fingers on the radar screen. Somewhere in my brain a knowledge base was placed on alert. In the ER the phone was transferred from the triage nurse to a medical student to John Benner, the attending physician.

"Chuck, wanted to give you a heads-up. I've got a fellow coming in from Peaks Island on the fireboat. Older fellow, initials B. P. Passed out maybe twenty minutes ago. Fell off some kind of wall—hurt his wrist, maybe a hip. The police called the fireboat; they're on their way. B. P. says he's your patient. Anything you want to tell me about him? Blood pressure's a little low at ninety-eight over sixty."

"Thanks, John. I saw him recently. Blood pressure was running low, and I cut his meds in half. Don't be surprised about his kidney function or CBC. His most recent creatinine was two-point-six milligrams per deciliter and his hematocrit twenty-seven-point-eight. Tell you what—check him out. If he's broken a hip, admit him to Orthopedics, and

I'll consult. Otherwise, if it's a medical admission, I'll take care of him. Okay?"

"That's an affirmative. Hold on, Chuck, hold on. The police on the scene are telling me B. P. thinks he's fine. Doesn't think he should come into town. We'll sit tight here. I'll let you know if there's any further information."

I was thinking, if Bud Perry remained on Peaks Island, I'd be up all night like a kid with a finger in a dike. This was not an optional transfer. He was legally blind, a poorly controlled diabetic, and had undergone bypass surgery and a heart valve replacement. "John, there's no question; he needs to come in. Can you patch me in so I can talk directly to the police? I mean, will that work?"

Officer Mike Bartlett came on the line. "Doctor Radis, can you hear me okay?"

I placed a finger in one ear and retreated to the edge of the pilot-house. "Mike, this is Chuck Radis. I'm on the ferry. What's this about Bud refusing to come into town? He needs to be transferred, doesn't he?"

"That's an affirmative, Doctor Radis. He was out cold, lying in the snow by the stone wall when we arrived. Somebody saw him drop and called the station. He's come around, alert, oriented, regular pulse, lot better now sitting here in the snow, but I don't feel right driving him home. I've already called the fireboat. We can't stay with him all day."

I tapped my finger on the radar screen. "Can you put Bud on?"

"Sure. Bud, it's for you."

"Bud, this is Doctor Radis. What's this I hear about you passing out and not wanting to come in to the ER?"

"It's happened before, and it'll happen again, Doc. I'm fine. More than fine. Nothing a cup of coffee or donut won't fix. These jaganuts don't know stable when they see a pool table. I'm stable." In the background I heard Officer Barter plead with Bud *not* to get up.

The captain turned around, both hands still firmly on the wheel. "The man's a big problem to himself."

Officer Barter returned to the line. "Bud's changed his mind. He can't stand without blacking out. Settled that. The fireboat is off the point. We'll transfer Bud to the wharf on the sled, and MEDCU can take over from there."

Down below, I found Kate playing on the bottom stair, fascinated by a chunk of mud lodged against the railing. I gathered her up and plopped down next to Sandi. "How did your telephone call go?" Sandi smiled mischievously and pointed toward a very pregnant woman. "Barbara Dilton. It's her second baby. We've been timing her contractions while you've been gone." Looking down our bench I waved feebly to Barbara, who gave me the okay sign. "They were going to get you if we needed to lay her down. Look, her husband is helping her up. They're so cute. Everyone knew but you."

Wrapping my arm around Sandi's parka, I drew her closer. "Everyone may know that, but I know something they don't know."

Kate ducked her head in between us and whispered, "Taco is inside Mommy."

Kate has the basics down regarding who has babies—mommies—and that they grow in tummies and has decided she has naming rights: Baby Taco, her favorite food.

As we slowed to round the state pier, the emergency fireboat glided past us. Through the pilothouse window, Bud waved from his wheelchair to the passengers on the *Machigonne* like a dissipated Santa Claus. A blanket was draped across his shoulders, and in his right forearm an IV was running. Next to him an unhappy attendant from Portland's Medical Crisis Unit, MEDCU, held a bag of saline aloft.

A jet-black cormorant barely shifted from its post atop a rotted piling as the *Machigonne* glided in to tie up. Although the sun had peeked over the horizon, the aging Casco Bay Lines ferry terminal was aglow with Christmas lights. Strings of oversized bulbs accented the sagging eaves. Outside the freight shed, a bundle of balsam firs, twined and compressed for shipment to Peaks Island, leaned against a stack of lobster traps. "The bench isn't wet. There's no puddle," I decided. I held Kate's hand while we shuffled forward.

"What do you mean the bench isn't wet?" Sandi asked.

"Barbara's water. She can't be too far along if her water hasn't broken yet. It could even be false labor. She might be home on the afternoon boat. They'll keep her for a while for observation; maybe put a monitor on her." I was the expert once again, spouting medical pontifications. The line on the gangplank stopped. "'Course, if it's late in pregnancy, maybe the best thing would be for them to stay in town. Second baby . . ." Sandra nudged me. Halfway across the gangplank, Barbara grunted and grabbed the handrails.

"Blow it away. That's it, blow it away," her husband stage whispered. "Don't push. Blow it away." Barbara was immobilized, lips puckered, resisting the primal urge to push that baby out. "Hold on. It's passing. Blow it away. It's almost gone."

A high school student behind us whispered, "Wow, she's going to give birth on a gangplank! Cool." Moments later, a quick-thinking ticket agent appeared with a wheelchair and wheeled Barbara Dilton down the dock to an ambulance—Bud Perry's ambulance.

I kissed Sandi and Kate goodbye. "This won't take long," I yelled over my shoulder. "I need to check out Bud and make sure he's stabilized. Meet you at the car." What I didn't see was Kate crying when Sandi explained that Daddy needed to see someone who was sick.

My intent was to send Barbara's ambulance on its way and to quickly assess Bud as he came off the fireboat and call for another ambulance; if I'd learned anything, it was that Bud did not play well with others. At least, that was my plan. I stuck my head into the back of the ambulance. "Hello, Barbara! Good morning!" I smiled. "How are you doing this bright winter morning?"

"Doctor Radis! I thought I saw you on the boat. We were going to call, but I didn't want to disturb you. My husband, John, wanted to, but I knew we could get to town in time. I'm doing fine." She was between contractions, poised, fearless. "John is following in the car. I'm okay."

Abruptly, the ambulance door swung open. Bud Perry lay corpse-like across his stretcher. "I'm not going to ask you again; raise my head up. My back hurts." Bud's beefy hand balled up into a fist.

"Doctor Radis." The attendant recognized me. "Good to have you along for the ride. Mister Perry here got light-headed again on the fireboat. Had to lay him down. I've been discussing why it's important to lay flat. We've been in touch with the Osteopathic and ran in a good half liter of normal saline. Blood pressure is back up. Give us a hand here; we've got to move." Together we slid the stretcher into the ambulance, partnering Bud and my labor patient, head-to-head. In another moment we were racing across town to the Osteopathic Hospital.

"Barbara!"

"Bud!"

"What do you know? Seems like only yesterday I drove your mother 'round the backshore in the island taxi when she was overdue. 'Bud, break my water; hit that big old hole over there!'" As Bud rambled, I placed a damp cloth on Barbara's forehead. She moaned softly as a contraction intensified. "'Course, in those days, lots of those babies looked just like me. Not you, Barbara. Not you. And now it's your turn. By the way, where's your old man?" Bud pulled out his pipe and chewed on the stem.

Barbara let out a shriek, and the pipe exploded from Bud's mouth. Grabbing a deep breath, she white-knuckled the side rails and bore down. A guttural snarl spewed forth from deep within her throat.

"Don't push. Hold on," I pleaded, and rapped on the window. "Faster. Drive faster." Barbara grabbed a quick, decisive breath and bore down again. To gain more leverage, she reached across to Bud's stretcher and clasped his forearm, ripping the IV out. Blood and IV fluid soaked the white sheets.

I held Barbara's hand. "Hold on. Hold on. It's fading. We're almost there." Bud reached up and pulled his hat down over his face. Minutes later, we hit the speed bump at the entrance to the hospital and parked around the back. The MEDCU attendants swung open the rear doors, released the restraints on Barbara's stretcher, and whisked her into the ER.

Momentarily I was alone with Bud in the ambulance. I was shaken. Repeat after me, I whispered to myself, I am not a baby doctor. I am not a baby doctor. Bloodstained sheets lay crumpled on the floor. A dislodged oxygen tank was tipped over onto the bench.

"Take my blood pressure," Bud said.

"You'll be inside the ER in a minute. I'll be back later today. The resident, Doctor Murphy, will settle you in. Good guy. And Doctor Carol in the ER. You'll get along with him just fine."

"Take my blood pressure."

I took his blood pressure. "One-forty over seventy. Now we're getting somewhere," I added, thinking this would satisfy him. Instead, Bud

Perry suddenly lurched off the stretcher and scrambled out of the ambulance. Somehow in the rush he'd retained his white cane

Steadying himself against the door, he growled, "Now take it again." Bud extended his arm. I rewrapped the cuff and inflated it briskly.

"You're not light-headed, are you?"

"I've been worse."

Listening intently as snow drifted onto my face, there was: at first, nothing, but at 132 a faint tap-tapping could easily be heard. I slowly unwrapped the cuff.

"Well?"

"It's better than before—one thirty-two over sixty-two. The IV fluids certainly helped. How are you feeling? We'll get you checked out, and you'll be back on Peaks before you—"

Bud leaned on his white cane and abruptly turned his back on me. "I'm going home." A taxi driver across the parking lot spied Bud waving his cane. The driver pulled up alongside the ambulance and rolled down the window.

"Need a ride?"

"No, he doesn't need a ride," I snarled. "Bud, you're in no condition to go home." Before I could stop him, he opened the back door of the taxi, threw his cane in, and scrambled into the back seat.

"Bud, you could die! I mean it—get out of that taxi!"

Bud stuck his head out the window and tamped down a wad of tobacco into his pipe. Then he struck a match and took a deep, leisurely draw. "Had enough. I'm going home." Lifting his oversized watch up to his nose, he decided, "With luck I'll make the 9:45 ferry." The taxi made a wide, lazy turn before exiting the parking lot, heading west to the Casco Bay Lines.

I kicked the snowbank and spun around in frustration. To distract myself, I climbed into the back of the ambulance and gathered up the bloody sheets and replaced them with clean sheets from the alcove. Surveying the mess, I reached up and clamped off the IV fluids. A broken pipe lay up against the oxygen tanks. Forget about Bud Perry; the man is a major pain in the butt. I took a slow, deep breath and unclenched my fists. Think: Now, where's your green satchel? Concentrate. Okay, there it is, tucked in the corner. Knit cap? There it was, smeared with blood and amniotic fluid next to Bud's greasy pillow. I tossed it into the trash. I tossed Bud's pillow into the trash. I tossed the broken pipe into the trash. I felt for my wallet in my back pocket. Good. Keys? Where were my keys?

Shoot. The Children's Museum. We were supposed to go to the Children's Museum. Sandi had the car. I sat down on the curb. I didn't need to make this ambulance trip. The EMTs were professionals fully capable of delivering my patients to the hospital. I looked around the parking lot. No taxi. I rummaged a Snicker's bar from my satchel and stared dully at the ER entrance sign.

Behind me a silky-smooth voice called, "Hey, sailor, you come here often?" Sandi leaned out the driver's side window of our hatchback. Kate waved from her car seat, grasping the smooth corner of her yellow blanket, a thumb stuck innocently in her mouth. "Can you direct me to the Children's Museum?" Sandi asked. "My daughter and I are new to town, and we're lost."

I opened the front door and climbed in.

Sandi glanced into the open ambulance and raised an eyebrow. When I'd finished retelling the story—the blood, the IV fluids, the near delivery—I declared that Bud Perry was the biggest idiot I had ever met, ever, and that I was sorry. It was a big mistake leaving her with Kate and getting on the ambulance.

Breaking for the red light, Sandi leaned over and patted my hand. "I think you and Bud Perry are going to be the best of friends."

CHAPTER FIVE

It is a peculiar privilege of practice of a rural doctor to walk among one's dead.

—Kathryn Rensenbrink, MD

Outside of Richard Stack's room at the Osteopathic Hospital, I huddled with the family practice resident and two medical students. The resident presented her case.

"Mister Stack is a six-foot-one, three-hundred-six-pound male admitted last night from Peaks Island with a five-day history of fever, sweats, cough, and productive greenish sputum. He's a current one-pack-per-day smoker but until two months ago smoked between two and three packs a day for the past thirty-nine years."

"What was his room air O2 sat in the ER last night?" I asked. Making rounds at the Osteopathic was a welcome respite from the office. For much of my internal medicine residency, I'd focused on sick patients, and a morning of office patients with sore throats and coughs didn't compare to one sick, puzzling hospitalized patient.

"Eighty-four percent on room air, ninety-two percent on two liters per minute. Anyway, on exam, he's afebrile this morning, pulse eighty-eight, with a blood pressure of one seventy-eight over one oh two." She circled the blood pressure with her pen. "We've got to address that. Anyway, last night when I settled him in, he had diffuse wheezing in all lung fields with focal crackles in the right lower lung. Chest X-ray confirmed an infiltrate, Gram stain of the sputum showed gram-positive pairs of cocci, and his CBC showed an elevated white blood count and a left shift."

"His diagnosis is firm: pneumonia," she continued. "Probably pneumococcal. He had his first dose of Ceftriaxone last night. When the culture and sensitivities return, we can fine-tune his antibiotics. Nursing said he had a restless night, and fifteen minutes ago he kicked me out of the room before I could examine him—says he has a bad headache."

"Headache?" I asked.

"Yes," she looked down at her notes. "Every morning for the last few months he awakens with a headache."

"Okay, thanks. Good job," I said, peeking through the open doorway into the room. Richard Stack lay on his back, snoring heavily. I turned to the group and asked, "Morning headaches? Any significance in this setting?"

No replies. We filed into the room and circled around Mr. Stack's bed. The snoring was almost theatric—a rhythmic, prolonged, low-pitched, bellowing rattle, followed by a musical inspiratory wheeze. Up the scale, down the scale. Mrs. Stack, a third of the weight of her husband, entered the room carrying two cups of coffee and several donuts on a plastic tray. She placed the tray on the bedside table, and the group introduced themselves to her while she took a seat and added several packets of sugar to her coffee. In her open purse I noticed a pack of cigarettes.

Mr. Stack's breathing paused, for perhaps ten seconds, and then rumbled on. "That's it," Mrs. Stack said, carefully placing her coffee back on the tray. "I don't know what keeps me up more at night—the snoring or when he stops breathing."

I raised an eyebrow. The resident silently mouthed the words *sleep apnea*.

I had been reluctant to give up managing hospitalized patients when I'd began my island practice. Managing sick patients, really sick patients, connects me to my patients in a way that routine office visits for sore throats and coughs does not. And as a practice builder, working with medical students and residents at the Osteopathic Hospital and successfully discharging a complex medical patient also helped dispel any lingering doubts that an osteopathic physician was less capable than an MD. Of course, it helped that the DO specialists on staff at my hospital were always available to cover for me at night when a hospitalized patient crashed unexpectedly.

Phil Slocum, a pulmonary specialist, and Charlie Hoag, a cardiologist, were, for want of a better descriptor, nocturnalists, specialists who thrived at night on telephone coverage and emergency consults. No matter what time I called, they seemed to arrive out of nowhere, shaved, hair brushed, white coats crisply pressed. Without their steady backup, living on Peaks Island would have made a hospital practice impossible for me.

I sat down next to Mrs. Stack and reviewed where we were in her husband's management. "His pneumonia is already responding to the antibiotics, but he needs the oxygen and IV meds at least for a few more days. Before he's discharged, we'll need to assess a sleep study. The headaches, uncontrolled high blood pressure, fatigue—all of that can be linked to sleep apnea."

"I'm not surprised," Mrs. Stack said. "Have you seen him coming up the hill from the ferry landing? He has to stop and sit on the stone wall and then again on the bench at Lisa's and then again at the top of the hill to catch his breath. His face and hands turn this scary gray-blue."

"I have. And I've noticed that lately he doesn't even think about walking up the hill. Your truck is usually parked next to the wharf when the ferry comes in."

"I hope you can get him to stop smoking."

"That's going to be the key . . . for both of you. It's tough, but if you can quit, it increases the chances that he can quit. Whatever it takes—nicotine gum, a patch, willpower, prayer, hypnosis. You both need to quit. We'll start him on a nicotine patch while he's hospitalized and—" I felt a poke in my side. The resident pointed a finger toward the bed. Another apneic spell; Mr. Stack's massive chest lay still.

We waited. Mrs. Stack resumed drinking her coffee.

On the clock above the door, the seconds ticked off. Mr. Stacks lips turned a punky cyanotic gray, his blocky head perfectly balanced on two pillows, the covers neatly pulled up to his neck. Time slowed. Experience told me that at any moment Mr. Stack would commence breathing, but I whispered to the resident, "Just in case, go get the code cart from the nursing station."

"He's not, you know, he's not—"

"Go get the code cart."

I reached over and felt Mr. Stacks pulse at the wrist. Good. Not dead. The code cart rumbled down the hallway. Breathe, damn it. I took out my stethoscope and laid it on his chest to buy time. The heart was skipping beats under the influence of plummeting oxygen levels. This was *not* good. Then a sonorous inspiratory gurgle like a man trying to breathe with another man's hands around his throat broke the silence, followed by an explosion of convulsive hacking. Greenish phlegm sprayed out of Mr. Stack's mouth onto the bed sheets. His eyes remained firmly closed. A long mournful groan followed as he settled back into the sheets, fast asleep.

Mrs. Stack was the first to move. She shook her husband roughly by the shoulders. "Richard! Richard! The doctors are here. You've had one of your spells! Richard!"

He was awake now, seemingly in a trance as he sat and groggily swung his legs over the side of the bed. The resident lifted up the back of his gown and listened to his breathing with a stethoscope. "Better," she announced, her voice trembling. I noticed a wet stain under both armpits as she redraped the stethoscope around her neck. "Not great, but better. I'll come back later this morning, Mister Stack, and work on that stiff neck of yours."

As our little group moved down the hall, I took the resident aside and asked her to call Doctor Slocum, now. "That sleep study," I said. "Let's see if we can get it done today. And add thyroid function studies and electrolytes to Mister Stack's lab they drew today."

I turned to the medical students. "Our next patient is a legendary clamdigger from Chebeague Island who's suffered an unfortunate stroke. The guy was a machine. In his prime he could dig so many clams, he put four of his kids through college. Now, I'm not saying who I overheard," I looked at each medical student in turn, "but just because he has a feeding tube and a Foley catheter and can't answer your questions doesn't mean that he's not all there. He is *not* a gomer. We don't use the word *gomer* on this service. Got that?" There was a general nodding of heads.

Privately, though, I had deep misgivings about the case. Misgivings on how I played a role in his protracted misery.

When we'd first met at the Chebeague Clinic last fall, Jim Flats had already suffered a small left-sided stroke. Bent and arthritic from a lifetime of clam digging, he'd agreed to start blood pressure– and cholesterol-lowering medications but refused to go to Portland for additional testing. A month later, his family had found him in bed, unable to move, speak, or swallow. Following admission, a CT scan of his head, and neurology consultation, the diagnosis was clarified: locked-in syndrome. In such cases, there is paralysis of all four extremities, but mentation, hearing, and vision remain intact. Communication is limited to eye movement. There is little likelihood of improvement.

With only the most basic discussion with his daughter, I had recommended a feeding tube. In retrospect, he should have been allowed to die.

So that was my first mistake: the feeding tube. Next, a Foley catheter had been inserted through his penis. A hospital-acquired infection from an ulcer on his sacrum was treated with IV antibiotics. The months dragged by, the poor man uncommunicative, contracted, and unresponsive. Because Jim needed skilled care, and skilled nursing home beds were at a premium, he'd waited endlessly for placement. I'd seen him every day, a reminder of my poor judgment and inexperience. The family dutifully took the ferry in from Chebeague Island twice a week and repeated the question, "Will Dad ever get better?"

With each new rotation of students and residents, I related the same cautionary tale: When you're in practice, talk to your patients about advanced directives. Once a feeding tube goes in, it's difficult, if not impossible, to remove it. Think about the care you're providing, and ask yourself if that's what *you* would want, what your parents or grandparents would want. If only I'd discouraged Jim Flats's family from signing for the feeding tube, he would have died and received a proper eulogy and burial.

Forty-five minutes later, I pulled out of the hospital parking lot and glanced at my watch. It was going to be close. I hadn't made the 5:35 ferry home all week. Maybe I'd make the lights. Turning in to the Widgery Wharf parking lot, I knew that it was a ten-minute leisurely walk to the ferry, seven at a no-nonsense stride, five jogging clumsily in my work shoes, four in a shirt-tail-flying sprint. Locking the door of my car, I had a little less than four minutes to make the ferry. I resigned myself to the next boat but took off at a lope, hoping the ferry would be delayed.

As I stuffed my stethoscope into a back pocket, I pulled out my wallet, and a tattered round-trip fare to Peaks Island fluttered to the sidewalk. Reversing direction, I swooped down on the ticket, nearly upending a woman coming out of Gilbert's Chowder House. Accelerating past the fish market and turning onto the wooden walkway of Commercial Wharf, I saw a knot of passengers boarding the *Machigonne* for Peaks Island. Yes! I slowed to a walk and tucked in my shirt; I could almost taste the trip home.

A bottle shattered behind me. Half turning, I recognized a bare-chested fisherman from Long Island weaving his way toward the down-the-bay ferry. Spouting obscenities as he passed, he raised a hand, yelling, "Wait! Jerk heads! Hold the boat!" as another bottle slipped from his grasp. He grunted and bent down to retrieve the undamaged bottle, but another dropped, squirting ahead on the wooden wharf.

The last passenger boarded the *Island Romance*. Two deckhands started to slide the gangplank onboard as another released the dock lines. The crowd on the top deck of the *Machigonne*, berthed just beyond the *Island Romance*, turned en masse to watch the show. The fisherman tucked a bottle into his jeans, snared the two errant Budweisers, and, cracking one open, took a deep draw as he raced over the gangplank and disappeared into the hold.

In a wink, he was back and tipped his baseball cap.

Up on the top deck of the *Machigonne*, an appreciative Peaks Island crowd exploded in hoots and hollers. It was that perfect. The down-the-bay ferry eased away. By now, I was up on the top deck of the *Machigonne*, almost famous because I'd nearly been bowled over. A man I knew only as Larry—the guy with the brown Labrador retriever—handed me an open beer. "Hold on, hold on." He looked past me down the wharf. "We've got a runner."

Another fisherman raced down the wharf. Past shards of glass and vernal pools of beer, he charged, slowing only to scream at the bewildered ticket agent whose job it was to sit on a wooden stool and ensure all passengers were properly ticketed. I shifted my focus. Funny, I hadn't noticed what an unusually large, bald head the ticket agent had. Bone tumor? Congenital? Our runner stretched out his legs. It didn't seem possible, but he accelerated as he reached the edge of the wharf and launched himself toward the hold of the *Island Romance*, a good fifteen feet away.

Thwack.

It was a good jump—a great jump, actually. But it hadn't been quite good enough. He slid, inexorably, off the edge of the hold and into the water. I elbowed my way to the rail, transfixed, shifting into my what-if mode. Although this particular spring day was unseasonably warm, the water was a frigid fifty, perhaps fifty-two degrees at most. A life ring hung outside the pilothouse. The boat jumper flailed in the water, shaking his fist at the ferry as it rounded the end of the pier. Good—at least he can swim, I thought. The ticket agent picked up his stool and retreated to the confines of his booth, staring sullenly through the metal bars. It must be hard having a head that big.

And then a third remarkable thing happened: the *Island Romance* captain threw her engines in reverse and headed back to the wharf.

The jumper paddled over to a wooden ladder, oblivious to the ribbon of blood dripping down his face. Pulling himself up, rung by rung, the back of his jeans dragging below his waist, the sight of the ticket agent set him off again, and he lurched across the wharf and raged against the wooden booth. Then he backed up like a wounded rhino and gathered himself for a headlong charge into the booth. Someone yelled, "Leave him alone, you jerk." Paget's disease, I decided. The ticket agent must have Paget's disease; that's why his head was so big.

By now, the *Island Romance* was snugged up to the wharf and the gangplank made fast. Through the lower windows we could see the first fisherman slinging rights and lefts against a wall of life preservers wielded by the crew. The orange life preservers made for an effective riot shield, and they pushed him back, inch by inch, until he was in full view on the gangplank. The crew turned their back on him, but this was a mistake. The fisherman lowered his shoulder and sprinted back on board. We craned our heads, trying to see more.

There he was. He'd made it to the top deck. For a moment, I wondered if he would climb to the top rail and leap over to our ferry, we were that close, but he eluded his pursuers by ducking behind the smokestack and raced back down the stairway.

This time, the crew meant business. Four deckhands grabbed the fisherman and gave him the heave-ho onto the wharf. The captain gunned the engines, and the *Island Romance* was away, the gangplank half aboard, clanging against the hold. Police sirens wailed. The ticket agent shut the window blinds. The first fisherman lay in a heap. The ferryboat jumper collapsed down next to him and cracked open a beer. The *Machigonne* tucked in behind the *Island Romance*, and we rounded the Maine State Pier, heading for open water.

Up top, I moved toward the bow and found an open seat on a bench running the length of the inner rail. Along with the usual commuter crowd, the ferry was packed with visitors taking in the bay for the first time. A heavyset man with a bright floral shirt, unbuttoned midway to his navel, nearly dropped his binoculars at the sight of a harbor seal lolling off Fort Gorges. The seal popped up again closer to the boat before submerging, leaving a buttery halo of water marking the spot. Baitfish thrashed to the surface. Flashes of mackerel cut into the smaller fish, scattering them like dry leaves in every direction.

"Hey, Mister 5:35 Boat! I thought I saw you come on board." Sandi was at the top of the stairs, holding Kate's hand. Kate broke away and sprinted to me. I caught her under the arms and flung her into the air.

"So, what were you doing in town today, big one?"

"We saw an elephant at a store. When I grow up, I'm going to be an elephant."

Sandi settled onto a bench and dusted off the back of Kate's shirt. She adjusted her own blouse where it had inched up over an expanding midriff. "We went to the opening of Aubuchon Hardware, and they had free rides on an elephant in the parking lot. This girl is fearless. You should have seen Kate sitting up there. They wouldn't let her up there if it were dangerous, would they?" she asked as if reconsidering their recent adventure. "Anyway, when it was time to come down, the man had to pry her off the elephant."

"Daddy, when I grow up, I'm going to be an elephant."

"How'd the OB visit go?" I sat down next to Sandi and thought, Man is she getting big. Twins?

"Fine. The doctor took an ultrasound and said I'm about twenty-eight weeks. I told them, we don't need to know—"

"No, that's great. I mean, we don't need to know if it's a boy or a girl. There's one, right?"

"Daddy, when I grow up, I'm going to be an elephant."

"There's only one." Sandi straightened her barrette and rubbed my elbow. "Maybe we can take a walk on the beach tonight. When you're home this early, we should take advantage of it. With Taco on the way, they may need to tow me behind the boat, I'll be getting so large."

"Monstrous." I patted her tummy.

"Giganticus."

"Daddy, when—"

"Kate," I reluctantly turned my attention to her. "People can't be elephants."

"Okay. Then I'll be a horse."

"A horse?" I turned her upside down over my shoulder. "If you were a horse, then you couldn't be a sack of potatoes, now could you?"

Placing Kate back down on the bench, I noticed Ricky Hogan, alone, up on the bow. He'd made a slow recovery from mononucleosis last winter but I assumed was back running. Sandi wondered if he was still a member of the Boy Scout troop on the island. Now thirteen, Ricky was becoming a real concern. His mom worked part-time at Feeney's Island Market and seemed to be keeping the household afloat, but with Ricky and a brother, money had to be tight. Even in our brief time on Peaks we'd already seen several teenagers go off the rails. Ricky was definitely at risk.

As the *Machigonne* approached Peaks Island, I stood next to Ricky and, placing both hands on the rail, asked, "So, how's the running going?"

Ricky stared ahead, his face pale and expressionless. Even with his hooded sweatshirt on, he looked like he'd lost weight. I asked him again, "Hi, Ricky. Haven't seen you running this spring. You had a great cross-country season. Is Mister White coaching spring track?"

Ricky slowly looked up. "I'm running. I guess okay." He pulled on his school backpack and joined the line slowly moving toward the gangplank.

Sandi edged in next to me, holding Kate's hand. "Hi, Ricky. Thanks for mowing the lawn last summer. The grass is growing like crazy this spring. Can you stop by again soon?"

Ricky nodded, almost unperceptively.

Coming off the boat, I saw the police before they saw me. Big John and Mike shielded their eyes against the late afternoon sun as they scanned the off-loading passengers. Always serious, Big John looked downright glum tonight. Towering over the crowd, his enormous head craned forward, his hand rested against his forehead in an uneasy salute.

I was nearly by the two before I heard my name. "Doctor Radis, can we have a word with you?" Kate scampered on by, balancing her way along the rock wall up toward Lisa's Café. Big John dropped his hand down, but not before I noticed it was shaking. "Hi, Sandi. Can we borrow your husband for a few minutes?" Sandi released her hand from the crook of my elbow and looked at John quizzically before continuing up the hill. I could feel that stroll on the beach tonight slipping away.

The two policemen walked me slowly to the rear of the Jeep. Big John's eyes looked swollen. Mike crossed his arms and held up a finger to a woman carrying a bag of dog food coming around the Jeep. "We'll be a few minutes." For another minute, she stood on the sidewalk, waiting, clutching the twenty-five-pound bag to her chest, before shifting the bag over one shoulder and continuing on.

Mike turned back to me. "We've got a situation. Do you know Polly Sanders?"

"Sure—young woman, lives up Luther Avenue."

I held off, waiting for Mike or John to tell me what this was all about. Polly was depressed. She'd been laid off and was having trouble sleeping. She was rumored to have a cocaine habit. On the other hand, she was one of my rare Peaks Island patients who came in for treatment for depression and followed my advice. We'd had a productive visit, and she'd agreed to see a counselor in town. Some years ago, she'd told me that she'd gone through a previous bout of depression and that medication had seemed to help, so I started her on the same medication, Prozac.

At last week's follow-up visit she was sleeping better and told me her first visit with the therapist had gone well. She'd shown me a list of job leads she was following up on. I'd told her not to get discouraged if the first phone call wasn't successful. Wishing her luck, I'd penciled in a follow-up for later in the month. I remembered looking down and noticing that I was wearing mismatched socks—one green, the other navy blue—and that she'd made the same mistake; hers were green and yellow.

"Polly's dead." Big John looked away, staring back at the *Machigonne.* "Hung herself."

"She what?"

"Hung herself." Big John repeated. I slumped against the Jeep. Up the hill, Sandi paused at the corner by the candy store. I shook my head and she went on.

"Can you come with us back to the house?" Big John opened the door of the Jeep, and I climbed in, too numb to answer. We traveled in silence past the tourists milling around the candy store. John was forced to brake, hard, when Curt Flynn flagged him down and asked what the police were going to do about the teenagers skateboarding down Adams Street. Curt knew it was only a matter of time before there was an accident, a bad accident. Then what are you going to do? He wanted to say more, but John put the Jeep back into gear and told Curt they were working on it. Curt refused to pull his arm from the open window and walked along with the Jeep, repeating himself. "We're working on it," Big John said, with enough force that Curt drew his hand back.

We pulled up in front of Polly's place, a simple, two-story cottage with gray shingles. The front yard was recently mowed. The window box bloomed with marigolds, and along the property line a clump of Queen Anne's lace swayed in the light breeze. Mike walked up the walkway and opened the door.

"She's still up there," Mike said, half blocking the door.

"What do you mean *still up there?*" I asked.

"Inside," Mike answered. "She's still hanging. We called the medical examiner, and he said since it was an unwitnessed death, we need to keep the body where we found it." Mike swung open the door, and we stepped into the foyer. Directly ahead of us, between the kitchen and living room, Polly hung by a mooring rope from the hall rafter. Big John involuntarily made a choking noise and lurched outside to the Jeep.

Drifting through the door, I could hear the crackle of the police radio and in the distance the muted sound of neighborhood children running through a sprinkler. I couldn't keep my eyes off Polly's bloated face. Her lips were swollen, her eyes bloodstained. Her hands hung limply at the belt line, the thumbs pointing toward the front pockets. We stood nearly eye-to-eye with Polly, her feet dangling only six inches or so from the oak floor. It appeared as if she only needed to stand on tiptoes to relieve the strain of the rope. Beneath her feet, a puddle of fluid was already beginning to dry.

Against the wall was a table, and on the table was the classified section of the *Portland Press Herald* opened to the Help Wanted section. Mike went into the bedroom and returned with a wooden chair. Climbing up, he nearly lost his balance and lurched toward Polly, grasping onto the body for balance. He swallowed slowly and I noticed his uniform was moist across the chest. Pulling out a small notepad, he flipped it open and began to write. "Probably jumped from the table and broke her neck." He brushed the point of his pencil against Polly's jaw. "Look here: no scratch marks, nothing to suggest second thoughts. If you're dying by suffocation, instinct takes over, and the hands claw at the rope."

I shifted uneasily. A jumble of thoughts raced through my mind. Disbelief. Sadness. Anger. She had been getting better, hadn't she? Just a few days ago Polly had talked easily about her depression, how it made sense, what with her losing her job unexpectedly. But we had a plan: counseling, medications, support.

I imagined her hanging up the phone after another fruitless call looking for a job. She must have noticed the rafter a hundred times, but this time she pulled the table into the hallway and looped the rope over the beam. She could have pulled the rope down. The phone could have rung. Someone could have knocked on the door. Instead, she climbed up on the table and passed the noose over her head. She must have considered the distance. Too long of a drop and she'd need to pull her knees up until she passed out. She might be partially alive when they found her, and then she'd be even more of a burden than she was now. To break her neck, she'd need to jump up and out. Up and out.

And then she jumped. Even then, she could have thrown her arms above her head at the last moment and grabbed the rope, but she closed her eyes and sprung into the darkness.

Mike came out of the bedroom. "No note. I've searched the house. Nothing."

"Let's take her down," I said.

"Can't do that, Doc. We've got to wait for the medical examiner. Those were our orders."

"The woman's dead. I'm a doctor. I can sign the death certificate. This was no homicide; she hung herself, broke her neck. It's wrong, leaving her here like this, hour after hour, waiting for some doctor from uptown to pronounce her."

The more I stared at Polly, the more convinced I was we needed to take her down, now. Mike didn't reply immediately. He knew his orders were clear, but what were they going to do—demote him? Not likely. It wasn't as if duty on Peaks Island was the plum of the Portland police department.

"Blame me," I said. "Tell them I took the body down while you were looking for a suicide note." Ever so slowly, Polly's body rotated on the rope. Her eyes were on us. A shiver ran up and down my spine. "I'm taking her down. You can help me or not."

"John!" Mike cupped his hand. In answer, Big John poked his head through the door. "We could use some help." John tucked his head beneath the door jam, pulling on a pair of rubber gloves as he stopped short in front of the body. He handed Mike another pair and sucked in his cheeks, covering his emotions. I climbed up on the table to handle the rope.

"Take this." John handed me a rigging knife. "If you can't pull the noose over her head, cut the rope. I'll raise her up, give you some slack." Mike returned with a plastic tarp and positioned it beneath Polly's feet and rolled it out behind where Big John stood. John took a deep breath and, grabbing Polly under the arms, lifted upward.

I sliced through the mooring rope, and Polly's head nodded forward. The medical examiner would be angry enough as it was, I thought. This way, he could examine the neck without my fingerprints. While John held Polly by the back of her belt, Mike and I eased her onto a plastic tarp. It felt as if we were transporting a wet marble statue. But doing something, even the macabre act of cutting the body down, was better than waiting and watching. I gently closed Polly's eyelids. We withdrew outside.

Big John called town and found that the medical examiner was delayed. It might be the 8:15 boat or maybe the 9:15—hard to say. Maybe he should take the water taxi, John suggested. I looked at my watch and felt the pull of home. There was nothing more to say. The medical examiner could call me if he had questions.

"Do you want a ride?" Mike asked.

"No. I'll walk. Clear my head."

Instead of going directly home, I followed a meandering path across the interior of the island. The sun had set, but here and there the glow from a porch light showed the way where the path dropped off a hillside and passed behind a summer cottage.

The trail emptied out next to the Pond Grove Cemetery. Overhead, the tallest tree on the island, a ramrod straight white pine, shadowed the nearby headstones. I leaned against the trunk and watched a black-backed gull circle the graveyard and pass over the pines. Three freshly sodded graves held the remains of my patients. One held the body of an elderly woman with Alzheimer's disease, the next a summer resident who'd suffered a fatal heart attack not two weeks ago, the last my friend Sarah.

The woman with Alzheimer's had hung on for two long years after she'd lost her ability to reason or recall. She'd walked everywhere. With her passing, the family had finally been able to grieve. In her obituary I'd learned she had once been a third-grade teacher; a mother of four daughters and a grandmother to nine; a wife who shared her husband's passion for fly fishing; a meticulous, thoughtful woman who'd become, in her last years, all she was not. The death of the man with the heart attack froze him in time, just as he was: overweight, hypertensive, alcoholic. The night he'd clutched his chest after a last indulgent meal, he'd fallen with such lifeless force, the renters in the downstairs apartment had phoned the police. He was one month shy of forty-four.

I stood silently by Sarah's grave and remembered. When Sarah had learned that her colon cancer had spread to her liver, she'd told me it could be worse, and winked. For another month, I saw her walking slowly outside, but she soon withdrew to her bedroom under the watchful eye of her husband, Sam, a retired minister. Word spread that if you went to see Sarah, forget the moribund small talk; you'd better have a joke.

When she could barely lift an arm and had withered to under a hundred pounds, friends she hadn't seen in a quarter century made their way to Peaks Island. And over and over I heard the same story: I was afraid to go in her room. I worried I wouldn't have anything to say, but she got me talking, and before I knew it, we were both laughing. We were both crying. She made me feel better. I left the island feeling better than when I arrived.

The night Sarah died, the phone rang, and her daughter asked if I would pronounce her. On my way to the house, I'd wondered, why call the doctor and not the funeral home? Hers had been an expected death; there was no need to pronounce her.

In the kitchen, I sat with her husband, drinking tea. Through tired, swollen eyes, Sam said, "It's so nice of you to come." He explained that when she breathed her last breath, the girls had decided to wash her up and make the bed.

"Mother's greatest worry," Sam said, "was that she would die on our daughter Rebecca's birthday, forever ruining it. So she hung on. Tonight, well, we knew this was probably the night. She hadn't taken a sip of water all day, and her breathing was slowing down. Thayer—that's our son—was having a hard time. He went downstairs and turned on the radio to a jazz station. When he returned to the bedroom, Mother stirred, and we all leaned in to hear, who knows, perhaps her last words."

"I'm dying, and I have to listen to jazz?"

Sam's eyes had twinkled as he took a delicate sip from his teacup. Above us, there had been whispered voices and the sound of footsteps, padding back and forth. The faint sound of a hymn drifted down the stairs. The voices quieted. The house was still. Sam pushed himself up from the table and took my arm. "She's ready now," he'd said. "We'll head up and see the old girl. I think we'll both feel better after seeing her."

And I did, but not now—not tonight.

I lightly brushed my hand on the cool, moist granite of Sarah's headstone and wondered why I couldn't cry. A deep, aching fatigue washed over me, my mind returning to Polly and the awful image of her hanging. The questions welled up. Could I have done more? Could I have prevented her hanging? What if I had called her and asked her how she was doing? What if I'd worked more closely with her family? The tears finally came. I closed my eyes and rested.

Later, as I slipped quietly into bed, Sandi stirred and turned to me. "Big John and Mike dropped by. They asked if you were okay. I told them that sometimes you need to be by yourself. They left your green satchel on the bench by the table." Then we cried together.

CHAPTER SIX

Every drop knows the tide.

—W. G. Sutherland, DO

On the morning that Molly was born, I awoke with a different woman than the one I had gone to bed with. She was on all fours, panting and blowing, glowing with sweat. "Hi," I said carefully. Sandi was focusing into space. My words didn't seem to register right away.

"I didn't—" puff-puff, "want—to wake you."

"How long have you been doing, you know, this?" I asked.

"I don't know—a while." Sandi returned to her labors. Then it hit me: We needed to get to the hospital! I leaped up and pulled on my pants. "Are you alright? I'll call the fireboat."

The contractions passed. Sandi took a long cleansing breath. "Chuck, I'm doing fine. I've been timing the contractions; they're coming every five minutes. I think we should take the 6:15 ferry." I looked at her carefully. Now that she wasn't panting, she seemed like the old Sandi, cool, calm, and collected. She gathered her overnight bag, brushed her teeth, changed into a loose blouse, and, stopping at the foot of the stairs, doubled over, grimacing. I looked at my watch: it was too late anyway; the ferry would be here before the fireboat. I thought about having Sandi lie down to check how far along she was but decided against it. Gathering Kate up, I slung her over my shoulder and carried her downstairs.

A faint glimmer of light worked its way over the island. Across the channel, three lobster boats were already pulling traps. By the time we dropped Kate off at our neighbors and parked the truck, the sun was warming our backs. I unbuttoned my windbreaker as we boarded the *Machigonne*.

We lingered on the open deck. Sandi faced the sunrise and closed her eyes. She tried to hide her labor by pursing her lips ever so slightly and blowing away the contractions. Then her nose flared and her breathing quickened. I looked around and forced a smile at everyone on the top deck. Our neighbor up the street, Carl, drifted over and wanted to chat. "We've been watching. Wow. I mean, you're in labor, aren't you?"

Sandi's panting slowly dissipated, and she looked up, seeing Carl for the first time. "Hi Carl. How's Donna?"

"Fine. She's fine. Are you, I mean, is everything okay?" Carl asked, but before Sandi could answer, he continued. "Wow. You're in labor. I've heard about it—I mean, everybody has heard about labor, but this? Wow. Aren't there problems sometimes? I heard some woman died in labor at Maine Medical Center last month. and that's not supposed to happen nowadays, is it? Chuck, you're a doctor. What—"

"Carl, shut up," I said sharply. It was like I'd thrown a glass of cold water in his face. I thought he was going to cry.

"I'm so sorry." He turned to the upper deck passengers and announced, "She's great! Doing fine. Healthy as a horse!" He sheepishly scratched an ear. "Sorry," he whispered. Sandi reached out and clasped his hand, mistaking Carl's hand for mine, just as she began a contraction. Carl's eyes flared wide as a teacup. I grabbed her other hand and whispered to her, "Blow through it. Everything is going to be okay."

One of the crew notified the captain, and I felt the boat respond to the throttle. The Portland wharf came into view, and we glided into the slip, the deckhands scurrying about securing mooring lines and running out the gangplank. I pulled Sandi to her feet, and she walked unsteadily across the gangplank. From the Bay Lines office, another deckhand came running down the wharf with a wheelchair. Sandi's hair was matted, and her blouse was soaked in sweat, but she focused on a distant point and held on.

Our obstetrician nearly missed the delivery. In our haste, I'd forgotten to let the hospital know we were on our way. When Dr. Flaherty arrived, Sandi was in the birthing room, pushing for all she was worth. He smiled broadly at the two of us in exasperation. "Just like last time, Chuck. Nobody calls me. I'm beginning to get a complex. So, let's see what we have here." A nurse tied the back of his sterile gown as he pulled on a pair of gloves. Dr. Flaherty kept one eye on the monitor as he examined Sandi and didn't like what he saw; the harder Sandi pushed, the more our baby's heart rate decelerated. He reached up into the birth canal and felt a loop of umbilical cord coiled around our baby's neck. We went through two more cycles of contractions. Each time, there was a gradual, more worrisome slowing of the heart beat.

"Sandi, the baby is feeling some strain," Dr. Flaherty said evenly, "so we need to try something different. You'll feel more pressure this time with your contractions." As he spoke, he whispered to the nurse to set up for a "vacuum extractor." I stayed with Sandi at the head of the bed and saw him apply what looked like a good-sized suction cup to our baby's head when she peeked through the perineum. Then, applying a steady, even pull with the forceps, he held her position under the strain of the umbilical cord, even as the baby's heart rate plummeted on the monitor.

"Push, Sandi. One more push, and we'll have this baby born," Dr. Flaherty said.

Dr. Flaherty removed the suction cup and delivered Molly. With a cool, deft motion he uncoiled the umbilical cord from around her neck, clamped and cut the cord, and placed her in the warming incubator. In a whispered monotone I could hear a series of rapid-fire orders for suction and oxygen. A nurse stated, "Apgar at one minute—three." Over his shoulder I glimpsed the limp, pale form of our baby, and time slowed down. Dr. Flaherty tilted her head back to inspect the airway with a laryngoscope. A nurse handed him a straw-sized suction tube, and I watched as he aspirated a stream of creamy, greenish fluid from her upper trachea.

"Where's our baby?" Sandi looked up at me, exhausted but with an edge to her voice. "I was holding Kate by now, wasn't I?"

"They're warming her up. Every delivery is different," I said.

"Is she okay?"

"They're giving her some extra oxygen. She's going to be okay," I said, more confidently than I felt. "She's going to be fine."

Sandi waited another few seconds and repeated, "Is our baby okay?"
Dr. Flaherty said, "She's pinking up."

The nurse whispered, "Apgar at five minutes—seven." I began to relax. Seven is okay—not perfect, but a world away from three. And then a low-pitched, soft cry filled the room. It seemed neither a cry of pain nor hunger. It was tentative yet on pitch, as if our Molly were singing for the first time.

In the days and weeks that followed, life was even more hectic than usual. Kate accepted our new arrival, but on her own terms. She called Molly "Taco," as she had named her in utero. Our nights stretched out endlessly between the calls I received from the hospital and Molly's nursing schedule. We seemed to operate in a low-level fog, Sandi drifting off when Molly slept during the day, me resting after dinner, knowing that I'd be called frequently at night.

With Molly's arrival and the increasing demands of an island practice, I became, if it were possible, even more absent-minded. One day after a typical pinball day of clinics, boat rides, hospital rounds, and meetings, I sprinted for the 5:35 ferry, intent on not interacting with anyone. I boarded and took a bench seat in the hold, opened up the paper, and stuck my head in it. I desperately needed a break in my day, a time to check the sports section and mindlessly drift without responding to another patient or family member asking me a quick question.

Halfway across the bay, I glanced out the window. Hmm, we seemed to be awfully close to Little Diamond Island. Uneasily folding the paper, I scanned the bench and recognized no one. Peaks Island was a quarter mile to starboard. We off-loaded a few passengers at Little Diamond Island. Dang. I was on the *Island Romance* instead of the *Machigonne*. It figured. Cutting my losses, I stuffed the newspaper in my rucksack and disembarked at the next stop, Great Diamond Island. From the wharf, the second story of our blue-shingled rental was visible across the way.

I might as well have landed in Boston; if I waited for the return ferry to Portland and took the next outgoing ferry to Peaks, I would arrive home by ten. Wandering away from the ferry landing, I sheepishly knocked at the door of a nearby cottage and asked if I could use their phone, fibbing that I had just made a house call and they hadn't had a phone, and, well, I needed to call the water taxi. Something about the way the man looked at me made it clear he'd seen me come off the ferry five minutes ago.

The next day was Saturday, bourra day, as the day before had been bourra day and the day before that. This Finnish cereal mix of wheat, rye, and raisins is what Sandi grew up on, so it is what we do for breakfast —at least, it's what Sandi and Kate do for breakfast. The standing joke in our family is that a Finnish cookbook should be titled *Fine Finnish Food* and it would have a single entry: bourra. I like variety, and this morning I opened two cans of sardines with Louisiana Hot Sauce and poured myself a glass of milk.

Kate spooned in her bourra and watched with increasing fascination as tiny bits of sardine dripping in yellow sauce disappeared into my mouth. "Daddy, what are you eating?"

"I'm eating fish," I said, peering over the newspaper. Some people like fish for breakfast."

"I like fish, Daddy."

"But if you eat fish, we'll have to brush your teeth again," I added hastily. I didn't want my daughter to be a pariah. "These fish are called sardines, Kate. They're in a special sauce. Some people think it's too spicy. Your mother thinks they're too spicy."

"Can I have some sardines, Daddy?"

"You're sure?" Kate was very sure. Sandi was still upstairs, and I knew that when she appeared the idea of Kate eating sardines soaked in Louisiana Hot Sauce would be vetoed promptly. I spooned a small morsel of sardine into a bowl, and Kate eagerly placed it in her mouth. Her eyes flickered.

Now what? She smiled brightly at me, but I noticed she hadn't swallowed. Her finger came up lightly to her mouth and lingered there. Why didn't she spit it out? I went back to my paper and watched Kate pluck the sardine out and place it discretely under her napkin. An ambassador was born.

Moments later, Sandi noticed how hungry Kate seemed to be. "Isn't it wonderful how much she likes her bourra?"

On the two-year anniversary of starting my practice, it was a point of fact that I had examined everyone in the checkout line at Feeney's Market. I didn't mention this to Sandi as we reached the register. Ever the social worker, she'd analyze how I could "compartmentalize" my interactions with our neighbors. Frankly, it had never crossed my mind. Day in and day out, I'd stoically performed the intimacies of pelvic exams, palpated testicles and breasts, and checked for hernias and hemorrhoids. It helped that I viewed the physical exam much as an electrician impassively traces a faulty wire or a mechanic takes a look under the hood. Through numbing repetition, even the deepest probing had become no more invasive than looking in an ear or checking a mole. And people seemed to sense this.

Of course, there had been exceptions. The young woman examining melons in aisle two had come in several months ago with a cough and proceeded to remove her braless top before I could tell her I was going to lift up the back of her shirt and listen discretely to her lungs. Thereafter, whenever I'd see her in public, the image was replayed, and my face would suddenly flush, and I'd turn the other way. I just couldn't manage simple eye contact; the breach of social convention had been too jarring. With this exception, my relationship with our growing circle of island friends seems to accommodate the fact that I know a lot about them. And they, in turn, seem to know a lot about me.

I almost never shared information about patients with Sandi. This worked well for us. Early on in our marriage I found that if I reviewed the particulars of my day as we settled into bed it set my mind on churn. Instead, we talk about everything else. I usually slept well and awoke in the night for hospital calls with reasonable clarity and alertness.

My ability to take night call was in contrast to my favorite medical school attending, Dr. Richard Bond, a brilliant, caring internist in Kansas City with a burly white beard and walrus mustache. On my first week of night service as a medical student, Dr. Bond had instructed me to call him with the 3 a.m. blood sugar of a brittle diabetic in room 204. But first he'd wanted me to think hard about what dose I believed was appropriate. "Clear it with me first, but you manage the patient. It's how you learn."

So at 3:05 the lab tech handed me the STAT lab. The blood sugar was 296 milligrams per deciliter. I checked my cheat sheet. If the value was between 250 and 300, it suggested I write for six units of regular insulin. If between 301 and 350, I should give eight units of insulin. Hmm. 296 was nearly but not quite 300. Six units or eight? I'd go with eight. With a sense of exhilaration and trepidation, I dialed Dr. Bond's home phone number.

On the eighth ring, I became uneasy. Wrong number? On the twelfth, a wave of uncertainty washed over me. Just then, someone picked up the phone. "Doctor Bond?" I asked.

"Yes."

"Doctor Bond, this is medical student Chuck Radis. I have the 3 a.m. blood sugar for you." I placed my ear more firmly into the phone. Was I hearing a faint raspy snore? "Doctor Bond?" I raised my voice. "The three a.m. blood sugar? This is student-doctor Chuck Radis."

"Chuck? Chuck Radis?" he answered. "Chuck," his voice boomed. "I was just thinking about you."

"I have the most recent blood sugar. It's two hundred ninety-six milligrams per deciliter. I want to give the patient in room two hundred six eight units of insulin."

"Brilliant. Absolutely brilliant."

Sandi was home nursing Molly full-time and caring for our absent-minded, gangly daughter Kate. Housing on the island was cheap compared to the mainland, and we were looking to move out of our rental and buy a year-round fixer-upper. We'd joined a food co-op and befriended a growing number of young families with children. In general, we'd found that Peaks Islanders coexisted with reasonable tolerance. Last summer, a group of teenagers who'd begun verbally targeting two gay men living on the backshore were brought in line by the police and, more importantly, the general community.

But that's not to say we didn't have our share of controversies. One recently arrived couple decided they'd close the dirt road in front of their house because their property line extended across the lane. Big mistake. It was an even bigger mistake when they convinced a local contractor to place three couch-sized boulders on each end of the road and advised adjacent neighbors to stop cutting through "their" land. In the middle of the night, the stones were removed. The next day they had been replaced. The next night the boulders were gone. The back tires of the newcomer's pickup were slashed.

A notice had appeared on the bulletin board outside Feency's Market: *Meeting Tonight 7:30 Community Center: The Closing of the Road. Come Give Your Opinion.*

I'd dropped by the community center and squeezed my way inside as far as the hall fountain. All seventy chairs were filled, and a line of men, three deep and arms crossed, stood in the back, shouting down the couple's lone defender, who'd suggested that, after all, it was their land and we should compromise and reroute the road. The offending couple were nowhere to be seen. The city manager, all the way from Portland, tried to pacify the crowd.

While babies had crawled underfoot and beer flowed from brown paper bags, Peaks Islanders asked, If the town plowed a road for more than ten years, didn't that make it a public road? We had dozens of paths and dirt roads that cut across somebody's land. People coming out here lately are acting like you'd crapped on their porch if you so much as touched their grass.

And this: Even if it's legal, it's not right.

The city manager, gauging the tone of the crowd, had declared the issue needed further study but that for the time being the road would remain open, not closed. Traditional access would continue. Next to me, a man had shouted, "Don't even think about it. The road stays. End of meeting."

The next morning, I had pedaled my Schwinn steadily uphill, passing the island school where Kate would enter kindergarten the next year. A group of seven deer grazing in a flower bed barely acknowledged me. Last winter, several island families established feeding stations in their yards to "prevent the deer from starving." The following spring, twin fawns are the norm. Ten-foot-high deer fences are going up everywhere on the island in a generally futile attempt to protect gardens.

This rewilding of Peaks has reached a point where the deer are traveling in herds. I recently saw twenty animals grazing contentedly in an abandoned orchard pasture off the north end of Peaks as I ran by at dusk. The week before, a moose had swum over from who knows where and fed contentedly along the beach as a crowd of Peaks Islanders followed at a discreet distance. A yapping, pug-nosed dog had nipped at the heels of the moose. Moving back into shallow water, the moose turned and faced the dog, antlers lowered, until the dog slunk away. Then, entering deeper water, the moose had swum off effortlessly, its chest and upper torso breaking water like the prow of a sailing ship, until it had made landfall again across the channel at Great Diamond Island.

I parked the bike in front of the Gull, where Bud Perry sat in a folding chair behind a card table filled with packages of light bulbs. He wore a yellow Lion's Club vest and looked like he'd run a comb through his hair and (I did a double take) trimmed his beard. "Lion's Club fundraiser, Doc. Don't be a cheap sh—t; buy some bulbs. Between our lobster bakes and selling light bulbs we've raised seventy-five hundred dollars for college scholarships this year for island kids. By the way, I heard about Johanna von Tiling on Cliff Island. Tough break. Her neck surgery for that meningioma failed big-time. Those hotshots at the Mass General messed her up but good."

The word *meningioma* rolled out of Bud's mouth effortlessly. I wondered if the rumors were true—that Bud Perry had been kicked out of Harvard before World War II and joined the merchant marines.

Inside the health center, I settled into a stack of unfinished charts. There was a commotion in the waiting room. Bud Perry shuffled in. I looked at the appointment book and sighed. He chose an empty seat adjacent to the door and chewed on his pipe. In unison, the three women seated across from Bud pulled their magazines up to nose level.

"So, Sally," Bud started in, "how's your nephew John Seep doing?" Sally flipped to the next page of her magazine so hard she tore off a corner. "Heard he was arrested again last night for punching some guy in a bar."

"Bud Perry, John Seep is *not* my nephew!" Sally rolled up the magazine and pointed it at him like a cattle prod. "Don't be foolish. Keep your silly talk to yourself."

"Course he is."

"He most certainly is not!"

"You break the terms of your probation this soon after prison and, well, you know better than I do what that means." Bud chewed on the stem of his pipe and pushed up the brim of his filthy captain's hat. "Let me get this straight. Martha Maggett is your sister. Am I right?"

"Why would I deny that?" Sally shrunk back in her seat.

"Martha's married to Glenn Maggett, and they have, what, two kids? Those are good kids. Great kids. Course, most people don't remember that Martha was once married to Ed Seep when Ed was a sternman for Covey Johnson. Before marrying Martha, Ed fathered John Seep. Are you following me?"

Several sets of eyes peeked over their magazines.

"That would make your sister Martha, John Seep's—his what? Stepmother? And the way I see it, John Seep is your nephew—step-nephew if you want to get technical."

Kathryn appeared from behind the partition and motioned for Sally to follow her. Without a word, Kathryn rapped Bud over the head with the chart. A few minutes later I settled in with Sally for our regular visit and reviewed her recent blood sugars. The numbers were quite reasonable. I turned the page to her cholesterol results. Despite six months of dietary suggestions, her cholesterol level remained unacceptably high. She agreed to a trial of a cholesterol-lowering medication.

We sat for a moment in silence. I'd learned that patients often had concerns that emerged in the quiet of an unhurried visit. "Why is Bud Perry here?" Sally suddenly blurted out, scooting her chair forward like a young schoolgirl.

"I don't think I can share that with you. I wouldn't tell him why you were here."

She said she certainly understood but as she gathered her purse to leave said, "Well, whatever it is, give him a good dose of poison for me."

Across the hall, Bud Perry complained that he had a bum knee. "Sally and I go way back, Doc. I think her problems stem from repressed sexual desire." I said nothing as I flexed and extended the swollen knee. The ligaments were intact. There were no signs of a cartilage tear.

"Mister Perry," I reached into the shelf and located a jumbo syringe with a big-bore needle. "I need to take a sample of fluid from your knee. After I draw off the fluid, I'll inject a teaspoon of cortisone. It should help considerably." Bud's eyes tracked the needle back and forth as I emphasized the importance of obtaining a specimen.

Kathryn prepped the knee with an antiseptic before I punctured the skin and entered the joint and aspirated sixty milliliters of cloudy fluid. After injecting a shot of cortisone, I transferred a sample of the joint fluid into a green-top tube for a cell count and crystal search. Kathryn held a pressure dressing over the aspiration site. She grabbed Bud's cheek with her free hand and pinched it. "You are such a cutie! Now behave yourself next time."

Standing, Bud tried out the knee. "You didn't do a half bad job, Doc. You're no quack."

The remainder of the morning flowed well. Sore throats, coughs, pap smears, well-baby checks, bad backs, rashes. When I picked up Ricky Hogan's chart, I noticed that Kathryn had attached a sticker to the front: *Losing weight. Looks sad.*

I smiled and shook Ricky's hand as I opened his chart. "What brings you in today? Not feeling well?"

He looked past his sneaker tops and whispered, "I'm okay, just not hungry. My coach, Mister White, he wanted me to come by and get checked out."

I leafed through Ricky's chart. Five-feet-four, 120 pounds during his bout with mono last fall, 125 two months after he recovered. Today's weight: refused. To break the ice, I asked about the new Boy Scout troop on the island.

"Scouts suck."

"Well, they're certainly not for everybody," I replied evenly. "I lasted less than six months in scouting when I was about your age."

Ricky looked up. "What happened?"

"On an overnight camping trip, I decided to go out night fishing for largemouth bass. Thing is, the best bass lake was a two-mile hike from camp. Maybe I forgot to tell anyone where I was going. Anyway, the whole camp was out searching for me in the rain when I snuck back into camp at three in the morning. After that, well, the troop leaders decided I just didn't fit in."

A crooked half-smile crossed Ricky's face.

"Ricky, I want to palpate, you know, touch your neck, to gauge the size of your thyroid gland. Sometimes an overactive thyroid can cause weight loss. Can I do that?"

He tilted his head backward, exposing his neck. I slid my fingers around the trachea and felt for the soft outlines of the thyroid. Ricky swallowed, and I could feel a nubbin of normal thyroid tissue bob against my fingers. He pulled away. I returned to my questioning, but it felt more like an interrogation. "Sleeping okay? Headaches? Changes in your bowels? Abdominal pain?" To each question he gave an imperceptible nod, volunteering nothing more.

Finishing my exam, I was certain of one thing: Ricky weighed less than 110 pounds. Still unclear whether I was dealing with a physical or emotional disorder or both, I asked, "Are you eating less because you're not hungry or just eating less?"

He didn't know. "Coach won't let me run unless I get checked out." He stared listlessly at the floor. "I need to run."

I tapped my foot on the floor in a paradiddle, a drummer's habit I slip into at times of indecision. *Need* to run? Want to run—yes, I understand that. But *need*? I looked at Ricky, scanning for rashes, his hands for tremor, his palms for increased pigmentation for clues. My differential diagnosis was wide: juvenile-onset diabetes, hyperthyroidism, Addison's disease, occult renal failure, anxiety disorder, anorexia nervosa. Cancer? He could have cancer. It happens. Ricky held his arm out stiffly as I drew three vials of blood, wrapping them carefully in gauze to protect them on their trip to town.

I looked at him soberly. "I need to call your mom. Your coach, Mister White—would you mind if I talked with him? You're losing weight, and running burns calories." Again that imperceptible nod. "Is there anything on your mind—anything you want to tell me?" He didn't think so. He couldn't get out of the exam room fast enough. Through the window I watched Ricky push open the clinic door and slip into a jog down Sterling Street, his legs churning as he ran toward home. When the phone rang, it was Ricky's coach.

Coach White thought Ricky was anorectic. He suggested that we allow Ricky to stay on the team but that he'd carefully limit his workouts. He recalled that this had worked well for a girl on the team two years ago. "Of course, every athlete is different. What might work for one might not work for another."

I hedged and suggested we wait for the test results. Anorexia was uncommon in an adolescent boy, and other medical conditions were statistically more likely.

By midafternoon, I'd reached Ricky's mother, who wondered whether he had anxiety or maybe even depression. She'd noticed the house was often locked with Ricky inside when she arrived home after working the afternoon shift at Feeney's. The bathroom light was left on all night. Nothing she cooked for Ricky seemed to taste right to him. After picking at his dinner, he'd take off for a run and return home exhausted, drink a quart of water, and retreat to his room.

"Maybe there's a pill you can give Ricky?" she wondered.

The lab studies were normal. *Anorexia nervosa* settled in as my working diagnosis. For my part, I had zero experience in treating anorexia. Anxiety? Depression? I had some experience with managing both conditions. That might account for some of Ricky's transformation, but, no, instinctively I felt there was more to this than simple adolescent anxiety. The image of Polly Sanders hanging was never far from my mind.

This was one case I didn't want to manage solo. During my training I'd assumed that I could refer patients to a psychiatrist as easily as setting up a consult with a cardiologist, but I had been mistaken. The majority of psychiatrists, I soon discovered, consulted and managed psychotropic medications and left the counseling to others. That meant two separate office visits. Last month when I'd convinced a patient to seek psychiatric care they'd first needed to see a triage counselor at Community Counseling. Then the patient had been scheduled—based on an urgency-acuity index—for the next available social work counselor. Later, if a psychiatric evaluation were indicated—which was why I had made the referral in the first place—it would be called in. And then the wait would begin.

For the typical fragile, depressed, patient, this was a formidable gauntlet. How would I like to tell my tale of woe to stranger after concerned stranger? In my jaded experience on the island, only the people that didn't need psychiatric care got it; the rest fell by the wayside or ended up in the emergency room. What was equally frustrating was that I almost never received a copy of the consult or counseling sessions from either psychiatrists or social workers.

Were psychiatrists treating the whole person or only the part of the anatomy that opened to ingest a dose of Prozac? Throw in a ferry ride to town, and for most island patients I'd become their de facto mental health specialist.

But not for Ricky. I needed to get him plugged in to someone skilled in evaluating and treating anorexia. After a flurry of phone calls, I succeeded in scheduling a consult with child psychiatry at Maine Med, but it was six weeks off. I called back and asked the receptionist to place Ricky on the cancellation list. I opened my pocket calendar and wrote, *Review male anorexia.*

That afternoon, Sister Mia dropped by for a follow-up visit at the health center. As I joined her in the exam room, I focused on the most recent lab, her hemoglobin A1c, a three- month average of blood sugar control. Surprisingly, it was trending toward normal. I reached over and patted her on the shoulder. "Your blood sugars are much better. That's fantastic. Are you joining Sister Marie Henry on her walks on the backshore?"

"Yes," she said. "And what can you tell me about our Ricky?"

I raised an eyebrow. "That . . . well . . . he's a great kid."

"Sister Janice saw him racing through the waiting room. Something has happened to that young man. Of that I am certain."

I shifted on my stool, my stethoscope draped around my neck. *Our Ricky.* What manner of communal ownership was this? Sister Mia leaned forward in her chair as I listened to her heart and lungs. Now what? Stall. As Sister Mia tried to speak, I put a finger up to my lips and placed the stethoscope over the carotid arteries. The rhythmic, gushing flow reminded me of storm surf on the backshore. I retook her blood pressure and scowled. "Sister Mia, are you taking your blood pressure medications?"

"Doctor Radis, Ricky called me twice this week in tears. The young man can't sleep, and you're asking me if I take my medications? As God is my witness, I take my medications whenever I think of it." She shook her head and glared at me.

I was conflicted. On the one hand, talking with Sister Mia about Ricky was a clear violation of patient privacy. On the other hand, my mind drifted back once again to Polly Sanders. Maybe if I'd made an effort to reach out to her family she wouldn't have felt so isolated, so hopeless. If Ricky was already calling Sister Mia, maybe that made her and the other sisters part of his extended family. With an absentee father he needed all the support he could get.

"Sister Mia, I can use some help with Ricky. I've scheduled an appointment for him with child psychiatry. But it's nearly six weeks away, and he's on the cancellation list. The problem is that with his mom working at Feeney's Market, if Maine Med calls, Ricky would have no way of getting from King Middle School to psychiatry. If we need to, can you take the ferry to town and drive him to his appointment?"

Sister Mia gazed at the ceiling. "If you must know," she confessed, "I don't have a driver's license."

I knew it, I thought to myself. *I knew she didn't have a driver's license.* "The others?" I asked slyly.

"No," she glared. "None of us has ever had a license. But I can surely arrange for the principal to release Ricky into my care. As you may recall, as a former Catholic schoolteacher I am entirely familiar with school policy. I'll take a taxi from the ferry terminal, pick up Ricky from school, and accompany him to his appointment. I will be available at a moment's notice. Of that, you can depend on."

A horn beeped outside. I peeked through the blinds, and Sister Marie Henry waved to me from the driver's seat of the Saint Joseph's by the Sea Nissan van. The front left wheel lay squarely over a flowering azalea. The rear wheel seemed to be dragging a small fruit tree by the roots. I felt oddly reassured that Ricky was in good hands. He was a troubled boy who'd found a tireless ally. I rested better that night.

CHAPTER SEVEN

Do something for somebody every day for which you do not get paid.

—Albert Schweitzer

There are clinic visits and house calls, and then there are after-hours home calls. Of the three, islanders knocking on our door were my least favorite patient encounter, and not for the reason you might suspect. In the office I had the ability to run simple tests and dispense medications. On house calls I overcompensated by toting along every conceivable "what-if" medication.

Home visits were bare-boned. When an islander stepped inside our home, I had nothing besides my stethoscope, a basic first-aid kit with a few Band-Aids, and an extra otoscope I kept under the bed. When I look back over the years, the majority of my after-hours patient visitations were entirely appropriate. A painful ear infection, or worse, a ruptured eardrum, is nearly as hard on the parents as it is for the child. A sick three-year-old shouldn't be bundled up in the cold and taken into town on the ferry to sit in an emergency room with their parents on a Saturday evening, only to have to wait while a prescription is filled at the hospital pharmacy, only to cry himself to sleep in the ferry terminal awaiting the last ferry home.

Ear infections are easy; they're a yes or no proposition. At the kitchen table, I'd sit the toddler on their parent's lap, provide her with one of Kate's toys, and quickly peer into the ear. If a red tympanic membrane was visible, I was only too happy to unlock the health center, apply a few anesthetic drops to the ear canal, and dispense a bottle of liquid amoxicillin.

What I dreaded was a summer visitor with a complex history who knocked on our door with puzzling abdominal pain. This, too, was a yes or no proposition. Yes, I should call the fireboat, or no, we can wait 'til morning, reevaluate, and obtain blood work at the clinic. Reaching a yes or no conclusion was uncertain business and based on gathering a history and performing an exam. Once a visitor crossed the threshold of our home, they became my responsibility. Those decisions took time—a lot of time.

In such cases, I often erred on the side of caution and recommended transfer, but this too could be unpleasant and stressful. Some patients simply wanted reassurance that something serious wasn't going on. The evaluation of abdominal pain was particularly difficult for me. After an exam, I might decide there was a very low probability that the patient needed a surgical evaluation, but it wasn't zero, and missing a ruptured appendix or an early ischemic bowel could be catastrophic. In these cases, I encouraged the patient to go to town. Not everyone took my advice.

Then there was one particular home visit that spiraled into a near tragedy. It certainly pushed Sandi over the edge. After it was over, she asked me if I would go with her to marriage counseling. I agreed; it helped save our marriage. But we're getting ahead of ourselves.

Remember Richard Stack, my hospitalized patient with sleep apnea? It turned out his sleep apnea was the worst case that Dr. Slocum, the pulmonary specialist, had ever seen. The apneic spell I'd witnessed at the Osteopathic Hospital paled in comparison to the results of his formal sleep study. CPAP was recommended, but Richard felt a suffocating feeling when he wore the mask and ripped it off after thirty minutes. The ENT specialist recommended uvulopalatopharyngoplasty, an extensive surgical procedure to remove obstructing tissue in the back of the throat, but warned Richard that the recovery could be painful and prolonged. Still, the specialist thought this was his best option. Mr. Stack refused.

Because he was at high risk for sudden death, a tracheostomy was offered. Surprisingly, he agreed to the procedure. A hole would be created in his trachea and a silicon tube inserted. During the day, Richard could plug the tube and talk normally. At night, after unplugging the tube, his breathing bypassed the obstruction of his upper airway. The surgery was unorthodox but effective. A repeat sleep study demonstrated that his apneic spells were dramatically reduced. He was discharged. Everyone was satisfied with the result—except Richard.

The man had a massive neck. The tracheostomy tube pinched when he turned his head. Sometimes it bled. One afternoon, he coughed as he turned his head to the right, and the tube popped out. The soft tissues folded over the ostomy site, and the swelling caused him to be short of breath. Richard took the fireboat uptown to the emergency room, and the ENT specialist replaced the tube with a longer, thicker trach tube. This worked for a week. Richard coughed, the tube popped out. This time there was considerable bleeding. Replacing the tube was more difficult.

The third time it happened, at eight in the evening, Richard banged on my front door, hands wrapped around his neck, his breath escaping through the tracheostomy site like a hissing snake before he jammed a finger into the soft tissues. "Doc, frigging tube is out! Ain't going uptown this time!"

As blood pooled onto our kitchen floor, Sandi ushered Kate out of the kitchen and upstairs for a bath. She turned on the radio to drown out the shouting. Richard paced the kitchen floor. "I've had it. Doctor Payson had his chance. I was better off before he cut me up. Here, you do it!" He pressed the bloody tracheostomy tube into my hand.

"Richard, you need to go uptown. I am *not* putting that tube back in your neck."

Tears streamed down his face as he paced back and forth in our kitchen. "I'm not going uptown. I'm not going uptown." He was close to a total breakdown. I looked at the tracheostomy tube and the hole in his neck. My black bag happened to be on our dinner table. Inside the black bag I knew there was a pair of sterile gloves, some gauze pads, and antiseptic.

"Okay," I said gruffly. "Sit down, Richard. Let me take a look." He sat down on the bench. I applied pressure on the wound with a gauze pad. After a few minutes the bleeding stopped. I cleaned up the edges of the ostomy site and took a closer look.

"Doc," Richard whispered, "I'm sitting here until you put this frigging tube back in my neck."

"Richard, I've never fooled with one of these tubes. I'm not a surgeon, you need to—"

"Listen, there's a hole in my neck and a hole in my windpipe. How hard can it be? Just pop the tube through my neck and into my windpipe so I can go home."

I was unmoved. This was outside the scope of my practice. But looking him over, I realized he was close to giving up altogether. He reached up with a bloody hand and wiped a stream of tears from his cheek. Now he looked like he was going to war.

"Okay," I decided. "I'll try it once, but if I can't push it into your trachea, I'm calling the fireboat. Agreed?"

Richard rested his arms on the dinner table and leaned back, exposing his neck. I washed off the trach tube in a bowl of alcohol solution and removed my outer shirt. Then I pried open the soft tissues over the ostomy site with two fingers and gently probed the cavity in his neck with the flexible tube. In theory, the procedure was simple. There was a hole in the skin of the neck and a hole in the trachea. I needed to line up the two holes and push. But I kept bumping up against a fatty mass of blubber; between the skin and the cartilage of the trachea were at least three inches of fat.

"More pressure. You need more pressure." Richard grimaced and pushed back against the trach tube. Fresh blood dripped down the front of his chest. I straddled the bench, barely able to reach across his enormous chest, resting my forearm on his sternum for leverage and stability.

Once more I met resistance in the deeper tissues. I checked my landmarks, attempting to stay in the midline. Major veins and arteries lay to each side of the neck. Surgeons have this to say about bleeding: all bleeding stops.

I felt my way deeper into his neck like a safecracker, probing with my fingertips for subtle changes in texture or resistance. There! I felt an almost imperceptible drop-off. "Richard, I'm over the trach hole. The tube has a rubber flange on one end to keep it in the trachea. When I push it through, you need to fight the urge to cough. Ready?" He blinked his eyes.

I popped the tracheostomy tube through.

Richard lurched forward, his hands jammed against his neck, fighting the reflex to cough. He rose abruptly to his feet, sputtering, droplets of blood spraying the front of my T-shirt. But the tube remained in place. A gormless grin spread across his face. "I knew it!" he rasped. He capped the trach tube and shouted, "I knew you could do it! I knew it!"

The contents of a jar of blueberry jam and a stick of butter lay smooshed beneath his feet. A bowl lay shattered on the floor. One bench was overturned. Somehow blood had splattered the front of our refrigerator. A potted marigold and a glass of milk somehow were spared not six inches from where his elbow rested.

I found a rag in the bathroom and washed down the kitchen table. My right hand was shaking. I placed it in my pocket. "You still not smoking?"

"I'm doing what I can. It's less—a lot less."

"Okay." After washing his hands, I watched him slowly lumber up the path to the street and squeeze into his truck.

I stripped down for a second shower and stuffed my bloody T-shirt into a plastic bag before tossing it into the garbage. Sandi joined me as the bathroom filled with steam. "So, how did the exorcism go?" she deadpanned. She admitted that she had crept back down the stairs and watched my initial clumsy attempt at reinserting the tracheostomy tube. Growing up on a farm, she was used to a certain amount of blood and gore. "I didn't notice if you were wearing gloves. You wore gloves, didn't you?"

We stepped into the shower, and Sandi scrubbed my back in friendly, circular motions. "Chuck, I've been thinking." The scrubbing stopped. "Medical school was not so bad," she began. "Residency was difficult, but we managed." I turned toward her to see where this was headed. Sandi's cheeks were flushed. Her straight blond hair draped over her shoulders. She'd forgotten to take off her barrette. "Alright, at times I hated it. You may not have kept count, but between your elective rotations in medical school and residency, we moved nineteen times."

"Nineteen? Are you sure?" I asked.

"Nineteen. Trust me. Four weeks here. Six weeks there. So that's why it's so hard for me to get rid of our packing boxes. Every time I looked up, we were on the move again. When we moved to Peaks, I thought, okay, I can do this. Probably won't be permanent. Kate can do this. Molly was born into this. But lately, I'm not sure you can do this. Every day you hopscotch between Peaks and the hospital and the outer islands. You can't keep this pace up. You almost never make the 5:35 ferry home. You—*we* can't keep this pace up. Something's got to give."

"I'll . . . get more organized," I said.

There was an uncomfortable silence. We both knew that was a well-intentioned impossibility. "I don't know what to do. I just don't know," I repeated.

"Well, I think we need some help. Will you go with me to marriage counseling?" There it was, a straight-up request. Just like Sandi to summarize and address our problems in one clear, unequivocal sentence. My first reaction was, are things really that bad? My second was to think, yes, they are.

"Okay. Sure. Let's set it up."

"Good," she sounded relieved. "We have an appointment with Cindy Wilson next Friday. You'll need to leave your Peaks clinic an hour early to catch the ferry to town. Her office is on the Eastern Prom. Marcia can take Kate and Molly for a few hours."

Back in our bedroom, I opened my At-a-Glance pocket calendar and penned, *Tell Kathryn no pt Fri afternoon. Don't forget!* I uncapped a red marker pen and drew three arrows pointing to the entry. Then I closed the book and placed it in the shirt pocket of a blue oxford shirt I planned on wearing the next day. For good measure I hung the shirt on a hanger and hooked it over the doorknob. Before getting into bed I picked out a tie and draped it over the shirt. Just to be sure.

The next morning our toilet broke, and Sandi called Paul, the island plumber, who said he'd be over late morning. It helped that Sandi was on extended maternity leave from her social work practice to coordinate the nuts and bolts of our fragile household. I lingered at the kitchen table, drinking my second cup of coffee, mulling over our conversation last night. "What do you think about Kate coming with me on a couple of house calls this morning? She can bring her yellow blankie and stuffed lobster."

"You're not thinking of bringing her to Bud Perry's? The man's mouth is a sewer."

"No, no. This morning I'm scheduled to check in on the home-bound lady midway up Luther Street. After that, we'll cut through the path to Les MacVane's; he's back home from the hospital after his stroke. They're both close by. We can walk."

She considered this. "Sure," she said finally, brightening up. "That's fine. Molly's going down for a nap soon; maybe I can open up a book. You're sure it's alright with your patients?"

"Positive."

A few minutes later, Kate bounded up the hill from our house while I plotted out the remainder of my day. Okay. Focus. Two house calls, Peaks clinic hours, boat to town, round on three patients at the hospital, discharge one, home by 5:35 ferry. Kate drifted back to my side as we cut through Snake Alley. At nearly four years old, she had already picked up her first garter snake and declared, "Daddy, some snakes are the farmer's friends." She peered into the shadows. "We don't have poison snakes in Maine."

"That's right, nothing to worry about."

"And the wolves are . . . where *are* the wolves, Daddy?"

"There are no wolves on Peaks Island," I reassured her.

"But where *are* the wolves? Are they in Portland?"

"No. The wolves are far, far away. Like maybe in Bangor."

Stopping in front of our house call's front door, I prepared Kate as best I could for what she might see or hear, trying not to worry her about the details: Mrs. Jones would be in bed, and she'd look tired and wouldn't feel well. I figured this was more than enough information. We solemnly made our way upstairs to the bedroom. Mrs. Jones brightened at the unexpected visitor and sat up in bed as I adjusted a pillow behind her. I unwrapped her ankle where a chronic ulcer required a dressing change. Kate hung back, pressing the silky corner of her blankie to her mouth. Then she spied Mrs. Jones's calico cat, who allowed her to stroke her back while I performed a physical examination.

"Daddy, what's that bad smell?" Kate asked.

Without looking up from my work I whispered, "It's the cat. Some-times cats have gas, Kate."

She lifted up the cat's tail. "It's not the cat, daddy."

Next was Mr. MacVane. I explained that he was old and might look a little scary. Sometimes when people are sick, they lose weight. His hand wouldn't look quite right, but he always had chocolate chip cookies next to his chair. I rang the bell, and Mr. MacVane answered the door, clean-shaven but swaying to the side that had suffered his recent stroke.

I felt a tug at my pocket. "Daddy."

We moved into the foyer. Mr. MacVane was proud that this was the first day he'd gone without his walker. I complimented him on his progress but suggested that he stay with the walker a little longer. If he fell, he might break a hip.

"Daddy."

Mr. MacVane eased himself into his recliner while I made a list of home-adaptation equipment he required: a grab bar for the shower, a toilet seat extension.

Kate planted herself in front of us. Looking Mr. MacVane up and down, she declared, "You don't look very sick."

When we returned, Sandi was out in the shed with Molly perched contentedly in her backpack. Kate and I watched Sandi rummage through the hand tools. Then she smiled sweetly at us and asked Kate how the house calls went. Kate said, "I smelled poop and ate a cookie."

"Good job. Oh, Chuck, we need to buy more tools." She headed up to Paul's truck. A few minutes later she returned with a massive pipe wrench and laid it on the floor next to Paul, who was wedged between the toilet and the rear wall, trying to cut through a rusty bolt with a hacksaw.

Wiping her hands off with a grease rag, she said, "What fun! Paul's got the toilet working and showed me how to cut off the water main if one of our pipes freezes again."

I fixed a peanut butter sandwich for Kate and pulled Molly out of Sandi's backpack. She cooed and curled her head against my chest.

Outside our kitchen window, the tide was out, exposing mudflats and the sheen of eelgrass. Sandi pointed to a deer grazing on clumps of beach grass in front of our rental house. A loose dog came loping down the beach and chased the deer up toward the road. Last week, I'd seen the scene play out in the opposite direction; two dogs chased a heavy antlered buck down our path and across the clamflats before it jumped into the bay. I quickly dragged our dinghy into the water and followed the buck, its head and antlers gliding forward effortlessly as four tiny hooves churned below. Leaning into the oars, I could barely keep up. Reaching the opposite shore, the buck waded out of the shallows, shook itself, and disappeared into the woods.

I glanced at my watch, time for clinic.

The summer brought variety to my clinic days at the health center. There were the regulars—Bud Perry, Richard Stack, the nuns—and there are summer people. Summer people are not tourists; they often spend a week or more on the island, many of them returning year after year to family cottages. They volunteer in island organizations, the Library Advisory Council, Trefethen Evergreen Improvement Association, the Peaks Island Land Preserve, the Lions Club. And oftentimes they bring their unique and challenging health problems to the clinic.

Finishing a note, I looked up from my desk and saw an unfamiliar face in the doorway of the health center. Or, rather, a man so large that he darkened the waiting room as if he were a giant peering into a dim cave. From across the waiting room he boomed to Kathryn, "My dear woman, is this the facility for medical care on the island? I have a pressing medical problem that needs attention. Yes, immediate attention." Mr. Nicholas Strater wore a soft brown Australian crush hat and a burgundy dinner jacket over a peach T-shirt that declared *Chess: Where the Elite Meet.* But as he came closer, the spell was broken. Unshaven, his zipper at half-mast, he leaned against the reception counter and burped without raising a hand.

"I'm here for an evaluation. I seem to be gaining weight at an alarming rate, a preposterous rate. Two weeks ago, I weighed three hundred eighty pounds, last week, four hundred pounds. This morning, four hundred twelve pounds! Is the doctor in? I must have my blood glucose tested, but I don't need to tell you that—of course you realize my glucose balance may be perilously high."

Kathryn guided him into an empty exam room after confirming his weight. I extended my hand as I entered the room, all business. "Good morning. My name is Doctor Radis. What seems to be the problem today, Mister Strater?"

He shifted his weight on the edge of the exam table. "Yes, well, I'm here—excuse me if I don't rise, but my feet are killing me—I'm here seeking medical attention for a most distressing problem. I have gained nearly thirty pounds, and it's imperative that my blood pressure and glucose level be assessed. But I don't need to tell you that. Surely you know with all of this weight I'm carrying that I'm at risk for a medical catastrophe. It's really quite simple: I've been diagnosed with a cyclothymic personality and morbid obesity, and I must eat a carefully balanced diet. Unfortunately, somehow I've been remiss, and I seem to have come off my diet. Quickly, my blood pressure."

Without a word I wrapped his arm in the extra-large blood pressure cuff and slowly inflated it. The mere act of placing the cuff on his arm seemed to have a calming effect on him. With his free hand, he placed a mint in his mouth and took out a small notebook and pen, awaiting the numbers. Surprisingly, his blood pressure was perfectly normal. "Are you on any medications?" I asked.

"No, none that I'm aware of."

Pricking his finger, I placed a drop of blood on a test strip and ran his blood sugar; this too was in the normal range. I informed him of the good news. "Mister Strater, your blood pressure is one twenty-four over seventy-eight, and the glucose level is ninety-eight. Of course—"

"There must be some mistake, surely . . ." He pressed a beefy hand over his heart.

"That can happen. Let's see your other arm." This time I deflated the cuff more slowly and listened as if I were wrestling with numbers most difficult. I drew blood from a vein at the crook of his elbow and placed half the sample in a red-top tube for the hospital lab and repeated his glucometer assay. The numbers remained the same. I informed him of the good news.

"That is absolutely astounding! But what of the weight gain? At this rate, why, in a matter of weeks, I'll be unable to move! There must be a facility I can be admitted to. The executor of my estate will take care of everything. In La Paz, Mexico, there is a weight-loss clinic, but I don't have to tell you that; as a physician you must be familiar with their work. It is world-renowned. And of course, there were others—Duke, the Mayo Clinic. But I was successful in Mexico—quite rigorous, but successful. And now this."

Momentarily, we were both at a loss for words; then his eyes brightened. "Locally? Locally, is there a facility you can admit me to?"

Now, I am blessed with a poker face that holds me in good stead when I am thinking one thing and must say another. In my mind I knew I would never be browbeaten into an emergency obesity admission. On the other hand, I didn't think he'd be satisfied with a twelve hundred–calorie diabetic diet program and a follow-up visit in two weeks. I looked at him evenly, searching for just the right mix of concern and reassurance. Checkmate. We stared pleasantly at each other.

Mr. Strater begged the question, arose, and made his way to the door. "My dear doctor, you must make a call for me. Clearly I am in desperate need of specialized treatment. I'll return tomorrow for a recheck. You must promise to make the necessary arrangements. Here is my card." And he left without paying his bill.

Not thirty minutes later Anne knocked on the door. "Can you take a call?"

I looked up from burning a wart off the bottom of Eric's heel, one of our island policemen. "Sure. Just a minute."

At my desk, I picked up the phone. "This is Doctor Smithson, Duke University Medical Center, Department of Bariatrics. We've received a phone call today from a Mister Strater—a Mister Nicholas Strater."

"Yes. I seem to recall Mister Strater dropping by today. What can I do for you?"

"Good, good. Then you're his primary care physician?" I thought this over and admitted that, technically, that was true. "Good. Excellent. Mister Strater may have informed you that he has spent time here at Duke Medical Center—considerable time, I might say—for treatment of his morbid obesity. It's been a most puzzling case; we make great inroads while he is an inpatient, but no sooner is he discharged than complications arise." I looked at my watch and leaned backward to view the waiting room. Anne raised one finger and pointed to where Sister Mia was roomed and extended two more fingers to the nuns sitting quietly by the toy box. Three more patients; I need to move along.

"Doctor Smithton—"

"That's Smithson—Doctor Elliot S. Smithson, from Duke Medical Center, Department of Bariatrics."

"Doctor Smithson, I'm running behind this morning; I have patients waiting to be seen. Can you tell me what you need to know?"

"Yes, of course. Mister Strater has a cyclothymic personality, and we are concerned he might need hospitalization to get back on track."

"What exactly would help you decide whether Mister Strater requires hospitalization?"

"His weight. It often mirrors his general psychiatric state. Can you tell me his weight? We have a signed release from Mister Strater to cover these developments."

"I understand. One minute—let me find it here." I ran my finger down the brief outlines of his visit. "Okay, here we are: four hundred twelve pounds." I waited politely for a reaction and tapped the receiver. "Doctor Smithson."

"Oh my. I was making some calculations. This is really quite worrisome."

"Doctor Smithson, I really need to get back to my patients. Do you have a message you want me to give Mister Strater? He said this morning that he'll return tomorrow to be reevaluated."

"Is his executor still in charge of his estate?"

"I believe he mentioned that."

"Very good. Excellent. Most excellent. We'll need some preadmission paperwork, and you may need to assist him with transportation arrangements. I recall on one occasion we were waiting for him to arrive and he ended up at some clinic in La Paz, Mexico." Dr. Smithson stifled a laugh. "Imagine that—Mexico!"

Saying goodbye, I placed the receiver down, allowed myself a half smile, and steeled myself for Sister Mia. Opening the door, I was relieved to find Sister Janice and Sister Marie Henry inside as well. They were giving up their own visits to divulge important information; Sister Mia was cheating on her diet. I encouraged them to give me specifics. In a confessional tone the two sisters described secret caches of M&M's and Pop-Tarts, afternoon snacks of chocolate-covered cherries, home-made cookies, and cheesecake, and late-night refrigerator raids for ice cream and fudge bars. I shook my head in disbelief, as if this couldn't possibly be the Sister Mia I had come to know. "Is this true, Sister Mia? Are you off your diet?"

"Yes, yes. It's all true. Not every day"—the sisters' mouths dropped in unison—"Well, not constantly, not between every meal. And sometimes at night," her voice sharpened, "sometimes at night I am up merely to relieve myself. I have my lapses; I won't deny that." She crossed her arms and leaned in. "And there are other reasons why I am up at night, as Doctor Radis is well aware."

CHAPTER EIGHT

To find health should be the object of the doctor. Anyone can find disease.

—A. T. Still, DO*

It is the nature of a general medical practice that the next patient after a well-child visit may have cancer. Or that in the midst of a run of sore throats and blood pressure checks a devastating chronic illness such as multiple sclerosis or Wegener's granulomatosis will present with textbook clarity. A new tremor, a puzzling cough, or the simple question, "I've noticed this bump; am I okay?" hangs in the balance as I sort through a differential diagnosis. Will I offer reassurance or run some tests? If I am swimming in a sea of uncertainty, should I perform the workup or defer to a specialist? If I didn't know now, how will I know later?

The past four months had tested my mantra that if I kept focusing on a problem, a solution would present itself. But reviewing the medical literature on anorexia, reviewing Ricky's case with my colleagues, and referring him to "experts" in the field hadn't prevented a steady, inexorable decline. Ricky was in therapy with an anorexia counselor, Sue, who'd drawn up a "contract" between Ricky, his family, and herself. It outlined privileges he'd earn if he gained weight and the consequences if he lost weight. Sue carefully took a family history, looking for clues of dysfunction that might answer the question *why*.

And, of course, dysfunction was present. What family unit can withstand the focus of a therapist who sees every family relationship through the lens of the anorexic client? Pick a week, and the focus shifts.

---

* A. T. Still, *Philosophy of Osteopathy* (Kirksville, MO: A.T. Still, 1899), 28.

Even though the therapist tried to avoid blame, Ricky's mother simmered at the implication that Ricky would be okay if only Ricky's dad were in the picture. What was his relationship with his older brother who had sunk into a daily stupor of drugs and alcohol? Was Ricky taking drugs? And after every visit there was the unanswered question, why was Ricky so broken?

In the spring, we tried to include running in the contract. Ricky could run but not on the track team. Lose more weight and even this privilege would be taken away. When he dropped to under a hundred pounds, I supported the counselor's decision to link running with weight gain. No more running until he reached one hundred pounds. Maybe it was a mistake. I don't know. Since then, Ricky had missed several appointments in town, and when I met with him, he was never really there. He was drifting away like vapor.

Psychiatry said he had an anxiety disorder and suffered from major depression. Prozac, a serotonin reuptake inhibitor, was titrated upward without obvious effect. These things take time, I was told by the psychiatrist, who saw Ricky twice monthly for his twenty-minute medication checks. A child psychologist did the counseling.

The week prior I'd seen Ricky loping around the backshore in his sweat pants and sweatshirt. Passing me, where I hung back on a side road, it was his smile I'd noticed first, a flickering ember of contentment. No, I didn't believe running was the pathology. The soft, tensionless roll of his stride couldn't be merely a catalyst for burning calories. I decided, then, to take more control of the "contract." We would talk; perhaps I could link limited running to a more healthful approach to eating and inject new possibilities into our regular visits.

One day, opening the door, I saw Ricky with his hands held stiffly on his lap, his left wrist bandaged with gauze, and I knew instantly that the running had been a mirage, a moment of peace in a still-tortured young man. Ever so slightly he extended the left hand, and I unwrapped the gauze, lightly, to avoid pulling caked blood off the razor blade cuts. The cuts were shallow, and blood seeped from the superficial veins, sparing the radial artery.

It took more than an hour to make the appropriate calls, making sure that his mom understood the need for Ricky's hospital admission. Failing to connect with his psychiatrist, I was connected to a psychiatry resident at Maine Medical Center. "Can't we directly admit him to P6?" I asked.

"No, not really. He needs to come through the emergency room. All of the potential psych admits are evaluated in the ER. Most likely we can make adjustments in his meds and avoid an admission. Sounds like his dose of Prozac needs to be upped." In the background I could hear her munching on—what, an apple?

"He's gone through counseling, meds—nothing seems to be working. This young man is struggling. Don't you realize . . ." I stopped. This was a resident I was talking to, a resident who wouldn't even be the resident to evaluate Ricky for admission. I'd save my energy for the attending. "He'll be coming in on the 12:45 ferry. Here's my pager number. Can the attending give me a call later today?"

Of course, clinic hours went on. Amid sore throats and a run of sore backs, Ricky left on the ferry with his mom, and I realized after lunch that, temporarily, I had nothing to do. "Didn't you promise Johanna you'd make a house call today?" Kathryn said. "I'm asking because the police called and wanted to know when your last patient was scheduled."

"I told Johanna I *might* make a house call today," I corrected Kathryn. Johanna had called several times in the past week. The surgery on her neck had left her with weakness in one of her arms. A post-op infection at the Mass General required several weeks of IV antibiotics. She'd developed a pressure sore on her buttock. I was surprised she'd felt well enough to return to Cliff Island, particularly with winter coming.

"They happen to be coming by the public float in fifteen minutes. Can I help you get ready?" Kathryn already had my black bag packed and handed me a tube of Silvadene. "My cousin's sister, who worked in the hospital, gave me this. It was her ace in the hole for bedsores. Never failed."

"Thanks. Okay. The hospital knows where to find me; tell them to use the pager if they mistakenly call here. I can use the police marine radiophone or Johanna's home phone. Shouldn't be any problem." The image of Ricky, slumped between his mom and older brother, leaving the clinic, was fresh in my mind.

I moved along the busy sidewalk, catching a glimpse of the bay between storefronts and over fences, through open windows, beneath overhanging porches and swing sets. One week into fall, the sun arced lower across the sky but still lit up the bay in vivid primary colors. The afternoon offshore breeze was a few hours off, and the water was still except for the gentle wake of a lobster boat drifting out in a shallow vee.

"Doc, you still pushing pills?"

Despite the warmth of the early fall sun, Bud Perry leaned against the stone wall in a bulky down jacket and heavy work boots. I noticed he'd bought Velcro straps for the boots and taken out the laces since the neuropathy had spread to his fingers. "Is Lisa helping you with your blood sugar readings?" I asked.

"More or less. Listen, Doc—why don't you rethink this whole idea of Lisa looking in on me? Cleaning up, I can understand that, but . . ."

Between Feeney's Market and the post office, the police boat was tied up, waiting for me at the public float. I'd need to hustle. "Bud, let's keep going with the system we have. Ever since Lisa's been helping you out, you haven't had a blood sugar over two hundred." Bud cleared his throat and spat and pointed his pipe toward my chest, as if to argue otherwise, but I cut him off. "And when was the last time you passed out?"

Finding Lisa had been a stroke of luck. She'd succeeded by ignoring nearly everything Bud said and knew intuitively when to back off if Bud dug in. When necessary, she gave back double when he became a royal pain in the butt.

When he refused to take his medications, she brayed in his face, "Bud Perry, you either take this pill, or I hide your cane." As a lifelong bachelor, Bud was unperturbed by grime, and this had only worsened since going blind. His small apartment was a public health hazard. On a typical day at Bud's, Lisa tossed away moldy, half-eaten sandwiches or scraped jam from the countertop and didn't see how one man could be such a pig. A week after she arrived, the throw rugs were pulled up and

Bud's greasy pillow burned. She bought him a talking watch with one-inch-high digital numbers and gotten Paul the plumber to install a grab bar next to the toilet. But she also knew enough to leave his collection of pipes, meerschaums, briarwoods, Bengalis, piled like tinker toys on the kitchen table, undisturbed.

As I handed Officer Bob my emergency kit, I asked, "Do we have time for me to hurry home and pick up my daughter Kate?"

Bob sighed and glanced at his watch. "Doc, we've got to be back by 3:15 for the shift change. It's tight as it is." He turned his attention to a lobster boat off the point of Little Diamond Island where an osprey nested on the navigational buoy. "On the other hand, it might distract Johanna to see a child. That might be to your advantage. Give you ten minutes."

I handed him my backpack and jogged back to the truck.

Sandi and I'd had four marriage-counseling visits. Sandi spent the first ten minutes sobbing before she'd pulled herself together at our first session. It was completely out of character; I could count on one hand the times I'd seen Sandi cry. To be honest, it was scary. It occurred to me that our marriage might really be in trouble.

By the end of the second visit, our therapist seemed to have a good handle on what we needed to work on. For me, that meant learning how to say no. I might not be able to totally control my hours, but I came to realize that even though I believed I was efficiently moving through my day, I was spending an inordinate amount of time schmoozing: a few minutes shooting the breeze at the nurse's station, another cup of coffee in the doctor's lounge, a meeting I lingered at after most of the participants were gone. Not that I don't need time to unwind—medicine is stressful—but when I observed myself, my schmoozing time wasn't particularly relaxing or regenerative.

I resigned from my position on the Pharmacy and Therapeutics Committee at the Osteopathic Hospital and . . . nothing happened. My excuse was that I lived on an island. It only freed up a few hours in my week. What I began to realize was that saying yes to all things in medicine often meant saying no to family.

Many of my colleagues, I realized, weren't only married to the profession but found it an alluring mistress as well. Even in the space of my six years as an intern, resident, and attending, I'd watched a number of marriages self-destruct, not solely by the allure of infidelity—and there is that—but from physicians spending nearly every waking hour immersed in the culture of medicine.

And Sandi? The counselor focused in on her expectations. On the farm, Sandi's mom had rung the dinner bell at 5:30 sharp, and Sandi's dad, her brother and sister, and several hired hands had promptly sat down for dinner at 5:45. It had been a time to share news, laugh, pick on each other, and hear about school, a sick cow, or a broken tractor. It was a wonderful family memory, a memory Sandi wanted to recapture for our family. Our therapist wondered if Sandi could give up her expectation that our family would eat dinner together on a regular basis. If it happened, great—work toward it, but don't beat Chuck up if he couldn't reach that ideal.

And there was this paradox: The therapist recommended that I get out and run several evenings a week, even for fifteen minutes, to help me wash away some of the pent-up stress. That is, if I were willing to commit to freeing up Sandi so that she could walk around the island on weekend mornings. This was tricky. Kate, and now Molly, knew that when Daddy came in the door each evening, it was time to play. Sandi would need to prepare them for the fact that, that even though I was home, they'd need to wait a little while before we were together.

Reluctantly, Sandi agreed to this last suggestion. By getting out and running before a late dinner, I seemed to have more energy for Sandi and the girls. I began wearing my running shorts under work clothes and stole a run here and there during the workweek whenever a blank spot in the schedule opened up. Sandi, for her part, joined her friend, Gail, for a weekly walk around the island on Saturday mornings. Growing up on Peaks, Gail was the resident historian of the juicy history of feuds and grudges on Peaks.

I tried to be mindful of nonessential house calls. They took time—a lot of time. For example, was *this* trip to Cliff Island essential? Without a house call, could Johanna remain on Cliff without regular home visits? And how did one define *better-off*? If I were to narrow the discussion to *safer*, there was no question that a partially paralyzed woman, living alone, twenty-one steps above the high tide mark, an hour and a half from an emergency room, was safer in a nursing home.

I boarded with Kate. Officer Bob surged away from the dock and pointed toward the backshore. Kate held Eeyore by a long ear and sucked her thumb steadily as she settled into a lobster crate on a bed of life preservers. The *Connolly* sliced through the water without a hint of pounding or lurching. Bob handed me a Styrofoam cup of coffee, and I sipped on it as I tracked a skein of eiders aiming for Ram Island. Upon mention of Ram Island, Kate said, "Poop Island," recalling our recent landing there. The visit had ben ill-advised for two reasons: nesting birds should be left alone during breeding season, and eiders primarily feed on mussels and excrete foul-smelling guano—from a four-year-old's viewpoint, the mother of all poop smells.

As we entered the channel between Cliff and Hope Islands, lobster pots hung limply at slack tide, and a knot of herring gulls dove on a cloud of baitfish, driven to the surface by feeding mackerel. When the sun dipped behind a bank of clouds, I zipped up my windbreaker and tucked in behind the cuddy cabin. Kate awoke from her diesel-induced slumber as the bow bumped against the wharf and asked, "Is this lady sick?"

"Yes. She'll be in bed downstairs and needs help getting in and out of her wheelchair. But she has a dog, Midnight, who's very friendly." Bob pulled out a newspaper and stayed with the boat. Kate fell in beside me, Eeyore under one arm, and placed her thumb back in her mouth. At the crossroads we angled left past the tennis court and community center and paralleled the shoreline through a grove of red spruce. The bittersweet and Japanese knotweed understory of Peaks was replaced here on Cliff by roadside thickets of elderberry and lowbush blueberry. We stopped to gather a handful of the blueberries and munched on them like popcorn. Above us, a downy woodpecker tapped at the trunk of a rotted spruce and flapped away deeper into the woods.

On the edge of the hillside, overlooking the bay, was Johanna's home, Valhalla. A white railing rimmed the porch on the second story. Mounting the twenty-one steps, I marveled at the tenacity of her neighbors to deliver her safely back home. Then again, after watching Gerald

Tingley and his brother lug their mother out of the woods, these steps were nothing more than a speed bump.

At the door I reminded myself that Johanna, like Mrs. Tingley, might well choose Maine Medical Center, where I was not on staff, if she needed to be admitted. Like a chameleon, I shifted back and forth, assessing my island patients in terms of their expectations. Was I really their doctor? Did they have a "real" doctor in Portland for serious illness and the luxury of calling me when it was inconvenient to travel to town? I told myself to quit complicating things: listen, examine, diagnose, treat.

"Come in, the door is open," Johanna called from the living room. "Chester, leave the mail on the table. Not there, I went through that mail yesterday." Chester, a friend from down the way, smiled weakly in my direction as Kate and I entered through the kitchen. Kate extended a cautious hand to Midnight, who was shaking with delight at the prospect of a new playmate. Johanna wheeled herself past the piano to the edge of the living room and greeted me with a firm handshake. "Doctor Radis, I was beginning to think you weren't coming down today."

Johanna's face was pinched, and over her left eye she wore a black patch. Her long white hair was wrapped tightly in a bun, fastened by a series of pins and barrettes. The skin on her arms hung limply onto the armrest of the wheelchair, and she shielded her left hand, the paretic hand, beneath an afghan. I glanced down to her swollen feet, the soft tissue drooping over the edge of her slippers. Kate clung to the edge of my trousers. "Johanna, I've brought a friend—my daughter Kate. Kate, this is Johanna von Tiling." Kate kept her thumb in her mouth and wiggled the index finger in Johanna's direction. With a free hand, Kate patted Midnight, who lolled her tongue with pleasure.

"She might be careful of the dog. Midnight hasn't been around children in quite some time." Kate's eyes widened, and she withdrew her hand mid-pat. From my bag I took a coloring book and colored pencils and settled Kate on the floor by the picture window while Chester took Midnight into the kitchen.

For the next forty-five minutes, Johanna recounted her admission from hell at Mass General. The cast of imbeciles and incompetents was lengthy, the miscues inexcusable, the result horrific. As she spoke, I examined her hands and worked my way proximally, testing reflexes, sensation, strength, and tone. I turned over in my mind the differential diagnosis of lower-extremity edema and methodically listened to her heart and lungs and decided that the edema was likely due to venous insufficiency rather than heart failure.

Johanna allowed herself to be wheeled to the edge of her makeshift bed and called for Chester, who steadied the wheelchair as Johanna reached over and tried to slide onto the bed. Something was not quite right—the relationship between the bed and the wheelchair was not exactly so—and Johanna emphatically aborted the procedure. I asked if I could help. No, Chester was the only one who understood what was required.

On the second try, Johanna let out a grunt, and Kate looked up, startled, before going back to her coloring book. With Johanna on her side, I donned a pair of gloves for a closer look at the bedsore. The afternoon sun, streaming in from the porch, provided excellent lighting, and I estimated the ulcer to be no more than a half-inch across and barely an eighth of an inch deep. I was underwhelmed. Pink, healthy tissue was granulating in from the edges, and there was no underpinning or tunneling at the edges to suggest a deeper infection. I suggested that the ulcer looked to be on the mend.

"Can you imagine, a healthy woman like myself, admitted for neck surgery, which they botched, coming home with a decubitus ulcer that refuses to heal?"

"Johanna, now that you're home, in a familiar bed, getting adequate nutrition, this ulcer will almost certainly heal in no time at all."

A bony hand reached around to where I held her buttock apart. It grabbed my index finger and forcefully directed it into the ulcer. "Can't you feel it? The edge—it's rolled up, horny. Don't you need to trim the edge down? I can't tell you how many times my father said, 'No ulcer can heal unless it's debrided.'"

I felt my beeper vibrate and pulled my hand away from the wound. I'd forgotten Johanna's father was a physician. That explained a lot.

871-0251, the ER at Maine Medical Center. "Johanna, I need to call the hospital. When I come back, I have a special cream I brought with me that softens the edge of an ulcer and promotes healing." By the stove I found the phone and waited while the ER nurse connected me to Dr. Schwartz, the psychiatrist on call. I'd planned on stopping by to review Ricky's chart in the morning, but this was even better; we could collaborate on his plan of care.

"Doctor Schwartz, this is Doctor Radis, Ricky Hogan's doctor."

"Excellent. I'm calling to let you know we've decided against admission. These cases are difficult, but the team felt we can continue to best manage him as an outpatient."

"You can't be serious." I squeezed the phone. "Ricky cut his wrist this morning; another millimeter and he would have been into the radial artery. I don't think this was a cry for help, Doctor Schwartz; it was deliberate. Don't you realize—"

"Yes, of course. Any self-destructive behavior can be a harbinger of a more serious attempt, but as I said, the team—and, I might add, that included both our outpatient liaison and social worker—felt we could safely discharge him under his mother's care. In fact, we have a group meeting scheduled for tomorrow morning with Ricky, his mom, and brother."

"Doctor Schwartz, have you met Ricky before today?"

"No, I haven't had the pleasure."

"Then surely you can understand my frustration here. He's been in therapy since April, and there hasn't been a hint of improvement. In fact, week by week he's slipping backward, losing weight . . . and now, today, he's cut his wrists. What does a psychiatric patient have to do before they're admitted in this town?" There was silence on the other end.

"Yes, I understand your frustration, but the truth of the matter is he left twenty minutes ago with his mother to catch the ferry back to Peaks Island. Tomorrow we'll reconsider Ricky's care plan, but for now I really must go. Thank you for your input. Goodbye."

I sucked in my cheeks and carefully placed the phone into its cradle. In the living room, Johanna sat on the edge of the bed and opened her ledger. She peered at me over the rim of her bifocals. "Did you bring a scalpel to debride the ulcer?" Instead of answering her directly, I opened my black bag and handed her the tube of Silvadene.

She read the label. "Colloidal silver. Good. Very good. Before he immigrated to the United States, my father investigated the antibacterial effects of colloidal silver in Germany. You did know, Doctor Radis, my father was a physician? And to think they've added colloidal silver to a cream. Did you bring a scalpel to debride the ulcer?"

Turning, I looked at Johanna wearily. "I have a scalpel, but we'll try the cream first. The ulcer is healing."

"How do I know you'll be back? Why not debride the ulcer *and* apply the cream? That would make more sense."

I held her good hand and actually bit the inside of my cheek. "Johanna, if I debride an ulcer that doesn't need to be debrided and that ulcer bleeds and gets infected, I would feel terrible. It would be an iatrogenic infection. Now, I want you to apply the cream morning and night, and lie on your side with the ulcer open to the air for at least two or three hours daily. I'll come again if the ulcer fails to heal." She remained unconvinced but sensed I would not be moved.

As I packed my black bag, I said, "I know the injured nerve must be very uncomfortable. I could give you a medication to control the pain."

Johanna declined. The aspirin didn't help much, but at least it agreed with her. A stronger pain medication might make her drowsy. Could I guarantee it wouldn't affect her balance? No, I couldn't guarantee that. "Then you're not giving me a pain medication. What, trade a painful hand for a broken hip? No thank you." I suggested a diuretic for her edema, but she countered, correctly, that it might increase her urination. Did I want her lying in her own urine? She would have Chester massage her feet; that would clear the edema.

Kate came over and leaned against my knee, and I knew it was time to go. There was nothing more to say. We walked down the lane in silence. She remembered the berries and foraged deeper into the underbrush, returning with a purple tongue. Kate said that Johanna looked scary, like a pirate. What was under the patch? Was her eyeball still there? Was she a pirate? If she was a pirate, was she a good pirate or a bad pirate? I asked her if she was scared and she said, no, then yes. I told her Johanna was sick and having a bad day. Kate allowed that she did look sick and added, "They don't put a patch on your eye unless you're really sick."

As we reached the wharf, a dozen doves flushed off the rail and made a long, lazy loop before returning to their seats. The air felt damp and chilled. Kate threw a pebble at a rock crab partially hidden by a clump of kelp. The crab scrambled to safety behind a barnacle-encrusted piling. As we boarded the *Connolly*, a Band-Aid slipped from my bag and settled on the water before it rolled in the shore break and disappeared.

CHAPTER NINE

I've lived in good climate, and it bores the hell out of me.
—John Steinbeck*

That winter, sheets of ice formed on the edge of Casco Bay, gradually extending out into deeper water. Loons and red-breasted mergansers, buffleheads and long-tailed ducks crowded together as the remaining open water slowly constricted. A snowy owl—likely pushed south from the Arctic by a lack of food—appeared on the mast of a trailered sailboat on Luther Street, a mouse dangling from its beak.

Several months ago we'd bought a house on the beach, a hundred yards from our rental. Until late fall we'd been unaware the house had even existed, the property nearly hidden by a Sleeping Beauty forest of Japanese knotweed, alders, and climbing bittersweet. As the summer growth died back, there it was: the leaning chimney, the ancient yellowed asbestos shingles, the waterside porch hanging on by a lattice of reinforced two-by-fours. Sandi's dad came out to Peaks before we'd made an offer to look over our potential purchase. Eight inches of water sloshed in the basement crawl space. Upstairs a single outlet supplied electricity to a bedroom and bathroom. Neither the upstairs nor downstairs bedroom had a closet. I reminded him that, after all, the cottage *was* on the water. He grumbled that he had one simple suggestion, reached into his pocket, pulled out his lighter, and flicked it on.

On the night that skim ice bridged the two and a half miles from Peaks to Portland, our pipes froze. I awoke that morning and stood

---

* John Steinbeck, *Travels with Charley: In Search of America* (New York: Viking Press, 1962).

under the shower expectantly before slowly realizing nothing was flowing out of the showerhead. Sandi located the hair dryer and, setting it on high, aimed it at the bare pipes where they ran through a cabinet adjacent to our outside north-facing wall. It worked, and she was so proud of her success that for the rest of the day she wore the hair dryer on her belt loop like a gunslinger.

I left the house early in case the truck didn't start. It didn't. Pulling up my scarf around my face, I took off at a lope for the 6:15 ferry. A neighbor, the visibility through her windshield constricted by ice to an oval the size of a mitten, pulled over and offered me a ride. Once aboard the *Machigonne*, I settled onto a bench closest to the baseboard radiator and opened up a book. A middle-aged woman in a gray parka, orange pack boots, and a rainbow knit cap squeezed in next to me. Intuitively I recognized the body language of someone who wanted to talk. Her nose was running, and she coughed into her elbow. I shut my book and turned toward her.

"Doctor Radis, I don't want to disturb you, but I was hoping you'd be on this boat. I wanted to ask you about Hazel Towns. I drop off her mail and bring her groceries once a week. Poor thing, she keeps a hot plate on the dresser and a potty-chair in the closet, so I know she's capable of moving, but she seems perfectly content to spend all day in bed."

"That's very neighborly of you," I said. A disconcerting, tinny, at times hollow, clunking sound vibrated through the hull of the *Machigonne*. I peered out the window and saw a harbor seal resting on an ice floe. I scanned the crowd of early commuters. No one seemed concerned that the *Machigonne* was not an icebreaker.

"Well, she also has a niece who comes out from Portland," the orange-booted woman continued. "She looks in on her on Mondays and Wednesdays. But, so, here's another problem: lately she's been acting kind of strange. When she speaks, it's like she's talking in riddles. She laughs a lot. It's very odd."

"Does she have a doctor?" I was intrigued; I didn't have a clue what might be amiss.

"Doctor Radis, Hazel's house is directly across from the health center. Don't tell me you haven't heard about Hazel before now?" I admitted

I hadn't. "Cat lady? House witch?" I shook my head. "Hazel Towns hasn't been out of her house for years; she's what you call *agafornic*."

"Agoraphobic?"

"Exactly. Doctor Kenney, when he ran the clinic, checked in on her every three months or so. Say, you couldn't stop by and see Hazel today on your way home? I could leave the groceries in the breezeway and yell up to her that you might be coming by tonight. That way I could avoid giving Hazel this viral thing. If you didn't mind, you could put the perishables away. The refrigerator is down the hall on the first floor. Hazel is upstairs."

I rubbed my forehead, thinking. I was on my way to the hospital, then on to Chebeague Island before circling back to Peaks for evening clinic hours. Passengers around us gathered up packages and children, zipped up their coats, and trudged off the ferry. "I can't promise, but I'll try to stop by tonight." I opened up my pocket calendar and scribbled *HC Hazel?*

Before heading up the coast to catch the ferry to Chebeague Island, I stopped by the Osteopathic Hospital and discharged my only patient, Dottie Ford. Dottie had more or less risen from the dead yesterday, but—nursing had already called me twice—she believed, no, *insisted* that she was ready for discharge to Peaks Island that morning.

As a brittle, underweight, elderly diabetic, Dottie's management had been problematic. She didn't always eat regularly or forgot to take her insulin shot. Her blood sugars were all over the map. Dottie's husband, Dan, called the police when he couldn't awaken her the evening before. Arriving on the scene, the police had found Dottie unresponsive on the couch with a blood pressure of only 78 over 40. Dan refused to have Dottie transferred to the mainland. Officer Mike called me at home and sent his partner, Eric, to pick me up.

The police Jeep screeched to a halt in front of our house, and I clambered inside, stopping off at the health center to pick up my emergency kit. In one more week, after interminable lobbying, we would have a modern, secondhand ambulance courtesy of the city of Portland. I won't miss the jeep. Stashed upside down behind my seat was an unpadded, orange-plastic bed board with white canvas straps. It had no wheels or padding. It was one step up from a plank.

We'd pulled up to the Fords' house, a magnificent cottage-style oceanfront home looking out to Cushing Island. I ran up the front steps with my black bag and emergency tackle box. Inside, I took one look at Dottie and told Officer Mike to call the fireboat over her husband Dan's objections. Dottie was unconscious, one arm dangling limply onto the floor, her cheek and chin blanketed with drool. Her skin was cold and clammy, her breathing shallow and irregular. Dan whispered in my ear that she'd be okay if we could just get some juice into her. "Can you wake her up?"

I registered his concerns. Dottie *was* diabetic, and this *might* represent hypoglycemia, but she was also ninety years old. She might have suffered a massive stroke, a myocardial infarction, a pulmonary embolism, sepsis from an underlying infection, or a cardiac arrhythmia. I shouted into her ear; no response. I felt her pulse; it was steady but feeble. I pinched her arm; no reaction. Her pupils were equal and reactive to light. She had no pathologic reflexes. I pricked her finger and placed a drop of blood on a glucometer strip. Twenty-six milligrams per deciliter. Low—low enough for her to become unresponsive. I'd hoped that's all it was.

Unwrapping a glucagon tablet from my emergency kit, I was about to place it inside Dottie's cheek when Officer Mike said that they'd already tried that and it hadn't worked. Scrambling through the tackle box I found a vial of D50—a 50 percent concentration of glucose. At the crook of her elbow I inserted a small-gauge IV catheter and slowly infused the vial of D50. In the background, Officer Mike confirmed that the fireboat was on its way.

The first sign that Dottie was going to be okay was when her tongue disappeared inside her mouth and she smacked her lips. Then the hand that had dangled limply off the couch moved to her chin and clumsily wiped her mouth. Her eyes opened. "That feels good," she said simply, looking down at the intravenous infusion.

"Hi, Mrs. Ford. I'm Doctor Radis." I was all business. "Your blood sugar dropped so low you passed out. We need to watch you uptown; I don't know how much insulin you've had this morning, and the effects of the infusion may last only a little while."

"Doctor Radis, thank you very much, but I feel fine now, and I'm not going uptown. Look, I'm eating." She lifted up a saltine cracker and bit it in half. "You're very kind." Mucus and phlegm stained her sweater. Blood was caked on her forearm where I'd inserted the IV.

She tried to stand, but Officer Mike laid a hand on her shoulder. "Dottie, Doctor Radis was nice enough to come to the house. The least you can do is follow his advice. We don't want to come back tonight and find you passed out again."

Dottie considered this request, the trip uptown on the fireboat evolving into a question of etiquette. "Do I have to go in that awful stretcher?" she asked.

The morning after her ordeal, at the hospital, dressed and ready to go, Mrs. Ford now was awaiting discharge. Sitting down, I realized my socks didn't match—not by a long shot. I reached into my back pocket. Good; I had my wallet. Something told me I didn't have any money in it. No, I was sure I didn't have any money in my wallet.

I reviewed the blood sugars on her chart. Shortly after midnight her blood sugars had bottomed out again. She had been slurring her words but coherent enough to drink a glass of orange juice under the direction of the night intern. A fasting blood sugar today was a very reasonable 126. I agreed to discharge her but only if she cut back her daily morning long-acting insulin by a third, explaining that it was far healthier to maintain slightly higher blood sugars than risk another hypoglycemic event.

On my twenty-minute drive up the coast to board the Chebeague Island ferry, I found an extra ticket in the glove compartment. Good— maybe Albion could lend me some money for a bag of Fritos at the Stone Wharf.

My mind drifted. In the last six months, I'd had exactly two phone calls from Long Island. Perhaps I'd started off on the wrong foot with my clumsy initial meeting with the library council. The clinic room, which was to be attached to the school, never did get built. Still, I thought I'd built up a measure of goodwill when I'd visited an elderly Long Islander early last fall and diagnosed diverticulitis. On my return visit, she'd made a good recovery after a two-week course of combination antibiotics. Shyly, she'd asked me for a favor: She'd inherited an heirloom pair of earrings but never worn them. "I've never had my ears pierced," she blushed. "Would you be willing to pierce my ears?" When I was done, she'd been more pleased with the ear piercing than with the diverticulitis treatment.

Then there had been the house call on Long Island that hadn't been a house call. Thinking back, I don't know what I could have done differently. Still, I suspected my reputation on Long Island might never recover.

It began with a phone call to the Peaks Island Health Center. A fisherman was wondering if I could stop by for a house call. His wife and he had come down with a respiratory infection two weeks prior. She had recovered, but he had not. Lately his phlegm had changed to a thick, lime color, and at night he was sweaty and cold. I looked over my schedule and agreed to see him.

The next afternoon, I knocked on his door. He answered, his T-shirt soaked in sweat. I listened carefully to his lungs. First the left, then right. I removed the stethoscope from my ears and said, "In the left middle portion of your lung I hear crackles. You have pneumonia."

"That's what the doc in the Quick Care said last night in Portland. Gave me these pills." The fisherman handed me the pill bottle.

Silently, I handed back the bottle. "You mean to say—" I began, my voice rising.

"Listen, I'm really sorry I didn't give you a call back. I just couldn't wait. I've got eight hundred lobster traps sitting offshore, and I need to keep fishing. Bills've been piling up."

"Sure, I . . . I completely understand." I was already packing up my green satchel and zipping up my windbreaker. I just wanted to get out of the house and get home. Plus, I was pissed off. He or his wife could have picked up the phone. Even the simple act of catching the police boat, tying up at the float, walking up the hill, performing an examination, reviewing my findings, and returning to Peaks had added several hours to my day. And for what?

Still, I sensed that there was something seriously wrong with the fisherman. When you've seen your share of sick patients, there's a difference between sick and ominously sick. Glancing down at the side table, I saw an open pack of cigarettes. "Still smoking?"

"Nah, lost the urge with whatever this pneumonia deal is," he shrugged.

"Did the Quick Care doc take a chest X-ray?" I asked, wondering if lung cancer was hidden beneath the pneumonia.

"He did. He was very thorough. Chest X-ray, blood—the whole works.

I retrieved my stethoscope and asked if he minded if I listened again.

"Course not. Listen away."

Placing the diaphragm of the stethoscope over his heart, I heard a murmur. Each beat of the heart was accompanied by a low-pitched *whoosh*. I pressed my palm against his bare chest, and there was a palpable vibration—a "thrill," in the language of heart sounds. Nearly all heart murmurs with a palpable thrill are serious. On a hunch, I'd asked to see his hands. There, beneath the third right fingernail, was a thin black streak, a splinter hemorrhage. Endocarditis, I thought. I ran my fingers through my hair and gathered my thoughts. "Listen—you haven't been diagnosed with a heart murmur before, have you?"

"I don't think. . . . Ugh, wait a minute, seems to me when I was a kid, I remember the doctor telling my mom I had a slight murmur."

"Well, I'm hearing a loud murmur now. It's what we call a *pathologic murmur*. It's very likely that the bacteria causing your pneumonia has passed into your circulation and infected the heart valve—probably the mitral valve. That's much more serious than pneumonia alone." I let this sink in. The fisherman stared blankly at me; I wasn't sure he'd fully understood.

"I think you should come in with me and be hospitalized. I'm worried about you. You need an ultrasound of your heart and cultures of your blood to assess whether your heart valve is infected, but at the very least you need to be switched over to intravenous antibiotics."

I stopped, assessing his reaction. His wife had drifted into the room and sat on the couch. She'd been listening from the kitchen. He looked down at his slippers. "Well, I appreciate that, but I think I'm already feeling a little better after my third dose of antibiotics today. Doc said it might take me a day or so before I turned the corner." It was then that I'd realized I wasn't his doctor; the Quick Care doctor was.

The fisherman hadn't been asking for a second opinion, but I'd been giving it. There'd been no moving him. I'd walked slowly down the hill to the police boat.

Two nights later, the fisherman was evacuated by fireboat to Maine Medical Center. In the ensuing weeks I heard snippets of information from friends down the bay. The fisherman's heart valve was infected. He was in kidney failure. He was on dialysis. He was taken to surgery for emergency valve replacement. He was on a ventilator. He coded. He died.

I don't usually share patient stories with Sandi, but this was different, and it wore on me. The end result was tragic and possibly preventable. And this: unless the fisherman's wife said otherwise, all people knew was that I had tied up at the Long Island wharf for a house call and the next thing they knew the unlucky fisherman was taken off the island by rescue boat and died.

But today I had work to do. By the time I pulled into the parking lot to board the Chebeague ferry, snow was drifting steadily down. The parking lot attendant was nowhere to be seen, but I hung my parking medallion from my rearview mirror just in case. Angling in to the wharf, the ferry churned through a mixture of icy slush where a Coast Guard cutter had recently cleared the channel.

On board the ferry, the captain invited me up to the pilothouse and explained it wasn't all that unusual for the bay between Littlejohn and Chebeague to freeze solid. "It's shallower and more protected than the outer bay. We adjust; doesn't last forever. Say, I heard this morning that skim ice formed all the way from Peaks to Portland. Now that's unusual."

Since I was the only one on board, I helped Captain Donny tie up the ferry at the Stone Wharf and from there drove a borrowed truck to the clinic at the public safety building. Inside was a young man with a laceration. He'd been splitting wood behind the house not fifteen minutes before when a good-sized chunk had come whistling by his ear and torn into his scalp. I injected lidocaine with epinephrine into the edges of the wound and waited for the anesthesia to take effect.

After cleaning up the wound, I probed beneath the laceration to ensure it was free of debris and, following this, set out my suturing kit. My mind slowed as I focused on my work. Most internists don't have the opportunity or background to repair lacerations. Outside of a month or two in the emergency room or holding retractors in surgery, our training focuses almost exclusively on the nonsurgical aspects of medicine. Thankfully, when I learned that my public-health placement would be on the Casco Bay islands, I'd picked up several elective rotations in the emergency room to round out my training. It had come in handy.

Suturing is satisfying in a way that the management of diabetes or heart disease is not. For example, this morning I made a change in Dottie Ford's insulin dose. In the coming months, if she stopped having hypoglycemic episodes, it was unlikely she'd attribute her stability to the lower insulin. She'd just go on living her life. Patients were rarely grateful for what didn't happen to them.

But repairing a laceration? Patients appreciated the final result; a gaping wound became a clean, simple line. Evaluate the wound, clean the wound, and suture the wound. How cool was that?

Snow fell steadily outside as I evaluated and treated a steady stream of patients. Albion Miller came by for a blood pressure check. A fisherman with an infected hand required antibiotics. A woman with postpartum depression asked if I could make a referral to a therapist on the mainland. A painful back, a painful shoulder, and a painful wrist, followed by a case of bronchitis, rounded out my morning on Chebeague Island.

Reversing direction, I arrived back on Peaks on the 2:15 ferry. I looked at my watch; I had time for dinner before evening clinic. Up the walkway, there was Sandi in the back of Paul the plumber's van filling a bucket with tools. She wore a pair of faded coveralls and an ancient pink parka. Hopping off the truck she pulled back her hood and gave me a hug.

"Hi, honey! Guess what! Paul asked me if I wanted a job! After you left this morning, the pipes under the sink froze. Now we have the pipes unfrozen and Molly's down for a nap. Kate is playing with her friend Amy at Marcia's house. We've installed heat tape around the feeder pipes; that should take care of the pipes until we can insulate the crawl space better. I feel like I'm back on the farm. Paul says I can work three six-hour days a week, and Marcia's agreed to watch Kate and Molly on a regular schedule. What do you think?"

"I . . . I . . . think that's great!" I stammered.

Sandi looked radiantly dirty and positively happy. One cheek was smudged with grease. I reached over to help her lug the bucket toward the house. "No, no—I need to build myself up," she said, taking the bucket back. "If I'm going to be a plumber's assistant, I need to get stronger. Do you need to go for a run before clinic?"

I did. Changing quickly into a pair of sweats, my head swirling with questions, I headed back up the hill. Despite the snow, the footing was firm. There was no mistaking how happy Sandi appeared to be in her new job. Working on the island certainly made it easier for her to respond if Kate or Molly needed help. She was strong. She could do the work, and with the prices Paul charged, he could afford to pay a good wage.

Coming up Central Avenue, I saw Sister Janice and Sister Marie Henry swinging their arms in unison, chatting away with Sister Mia, who lagged behind. I discreetly slipped down a side street.

"Doctor Radis, may I have a word for you." There was no mistaking that voice, but I was far enough away to ignore Sister Mia's call. My legs ached to pick up the pace and move into the trail system of the island's interior.

"Doctor Radis, a word please," Sister Mia called out again. I exhaled heavily and dutifully jogged back. "I hope I'm not disturbing your run."

"No," I lied.

Sister Janice and Marie Henry went on. "Doctor Radis, I know I'm disturbing your run." Sister Mia stopped and leaned heavily against a parked car. "But I knew you would want to know. Ricky was staying at his aunt's in Portland when he cut himself again. Apparently he nearly bled out. He required surgery at Maine Medical Center to repair the damage." Pulling back the brown cuff of her habit, she exposed her wrist and pulled a long, bony finger across the crease. "Today they transferred him to the Augusta Mental Health Institute. Here I thought we were making some progress . . ."

I felt an involuntary shiver and looked away, unable to answer. AMHI was a locked facility with a reputation as a holding ground for patients judged to be a danger to themselves or to the community. It was the only mental hospital in the state where the criminally insane were housed and was chronically understaffed and underfunded. Ricky could ultimately end up being discharged in worse shape than when he went in.

We walked on. "In the dead of night, he called and wanted to talk," Sister Mia continued. "The boy thinks he's alone. I tell him, no, God abandons no one." She looked up to where the other sisters waited. "This is enough for today. Has he called you?"

"No. Never."

I ran. I worked the hill up to Tolman Heights and pushed past the barn, deeper into the island's interior. A pair of deer leaped up from where they rested beside the road and exploded into the underbrush. I accelerated, and my breath came rushing in deep gulps, the sweat pooling over my eyes and dripping down my cheeks. Clumps of snow blew off the trees. I could barely see. On a long straightaway I felt my mind empty out. Exhausted, I turned around and made my way back to the house and changed for clinic.

Inside the health center I kicked my boots off and slipped into a pair of loafers. Kathryn, the phone nestled between her shoulder and ear, placed a hand over the receiver and pointed toward room one. "The Amundsens. Syncope. With the snowstorm everyone is cancelling. Might be your first and last patient." I slid a blank prescription pad into my back pocket and entered the room.

"Doctor Radis. Thank you for seeing Bobby today. I hope you can clear up a mystery for us." Mrs. Amundsen, all business, looked down at a series of questions she'd written on a notepad. I stole a peek at

Bobby—the focus of this mystery. Tall and lanky, maybe pushing sixty-five, he wore loose-fitting jeans, steel-toed Red Wing work boots, and a rust wool sweater, the sleeves pulled up to the elbows, exposing a pair of sinewy forearms. He reached down and picked up his down vest where it had slid off the chair, moving with a smooth, almost cat-like grace. I asked him to tell me more about this so-called mystery.

"That's the problem," Mrs. Amundsen said. "He doesn't remember a thing."

"Well, that's not altogether true. I remember stacking lobster traps by the shed and coming inside, looking out toward Pumpkin Knob, and . . . and then . . . well, I guess that's why we're here." He shrugged his shoulders.

"And that's true," said Mrs. Amundsen. "I saw Bobby standing at the window and thought, he's such a sweet guy, so I reached up from behind and gave him a hug. I stood on my tiptoes and gave him a squeeze; it wasn't anything like a bear hug—more like a little hug around the neck. Well, the next thing I know, *Timber!* Bobby falls backward like a sack of potatoes right on top of me! I said, '*Honey!* You're crushing me!' He didn't say a thing. Not a word. It took all my strength to roll him off. Then he came to like nothing happened. I said, 'Honey, you fell on top of me and nearly crushed me like a bug!'" She ran a finger down her notes. "Like a bug!"

I jotted down a phrase here and there to help narrow the differential diagnosis and turned my attention to Bobby. "So, now, walking over here, any light-headedness?"

"Nope."

"Any spells like this before?"

"Not that I can recall."

"Any warning before you passed out?"

"Nope. One minute I was looking out over Pumpkin Knob, and the next, Flora was shouting my name and we're like two teenagers on the floor." Flora blushed. "Probably never happen again. Just one of those things."

I looked up from my notes. "You didn't soil your underwear?"

Mr. Amundsen stared at me, openmouthed, as if I had two heads. "A man comes in with some kind of spell, and you want to know if his underwear is scuffed? Flora, this is why I don't go for doctoring." He reached for his vest.

"Bobby Amundsen, you stay right where you are. The doctor probably has good reason to ask you about your bowels." She looked at me pleasantly. "Of course there is, isn't there, Doctor Radis?"

I put the chart aside, and in my most somber, doctorly voice explained, "Some people black out from a seizure—not all seizures involve flailing your arms around—and they can soil their underwear." Bobby Amundsen raised an eyebrow, unconvinced.

"Irregular heartbeat?"

"Nope."

This was going nowhere. When all else fails, as the saying goes, examine the patient. Although Kathryn had recorded Mr. Amundsen's blood pressure, I repeated it while he was lying down and standing up. The same. Placing the diaphragm of my stethoscope over his heart I listened for nearly a minute. Like a metronome, the beat kept time at seventy per minute.

Lightly placing my finger over the angle of his jaw to localize where I should auscultate the carotid artery, I felt a vibratory premonition and heard Mrs. Amundsen shout, "There he goes!" Bobby's eyes rolled back, and he slumped backward onto the table. "You've done it! That's exactly what affected Bobby this morning." There wasn't a smidgen of worry in her voice. She adjusted the purse on her lap and smiled pleasantly at me. "It must be that spot up there you pressed. That's the spot."

At the wrist I felt for a pulse. At first, nothing; then Bobby's eyes flickered open. His pulse returned but at a turtle-like forty beats per minute. Abruptly, it jumped back to seventy.

"Flora? Something going on here?"

"You had another spell, Bobby," I said, "another blackout." Kathryn rolled in the EKG machine and calmly connected the leads to Bobby's chest and four extremities. Opening the emergency kit, I drew up a vial of atropine and a milliliter of epinephrine and placed them on the tray, just in case. I wiped my forehead with the edge of my sleeve, keeping one eye on Bobby and the other on the EKG tape. There it was— complete third-degree heart block, a definite indication for a pacemaker.

I pulled up a chair and sketched a picture of the electrical system of the heart. "Bobby, here's the story: The message from the upper chamber of your heart isn't communicating with the lower chamber. When this happens, the heart still beats, but it's in what I'd call an escape rhythm—maybe forty beats per minute, and that's not enough to support your blood pressure. This cardiac strip confirms the diagnosis. Kathryn is going to call the fireboat and make arrangements for you to be transferred uptown. There's no question; you need a pacemaker."

Bobby took all this in stride. One minute he'd been okay, the next he was wired up like a marionette and a strip of paper was telling the doctor he needed to go to the hospital. He ran his fingers through a shock of graying hair and rubbed his chin.

"Bobby, it's okay to scratch your chin, but don't rub your neck. Can you do that for me?" I reached up and gently pulled his hand back into his lap.

"If you say so. Mind if I read a book while we wait?"

"That's fine." I scrubbed his right forearm with a dab of iodine and punctured the skin with a needle. A flash of blood appeared in the catheter, and I advanced it into the vein. Kathryn handed me two strips of cloth tape, and I secured the catheter and flushed it with a vial of heparin. "Okay, heparin lock in, emergency meds on standby. Oxygen? It wouldn't hurt to start some oxygen."

Bobby looked up from his book. "Low tide in forty minutes. Full moon; should be a drainer." He mentioned this as if in casual conversation, but we both immediately knew what this meant. Bobby might not know much about pacemakers, but ask him about the tides and he'd tell you today's 11.6–foot tide—an unusually low tide—would drop the deck of the fireboat so far below the Peaks Island Wharf we'd be looking down into the smokestack when we began the transfer.

After parking the Jeep, Officer Mike and Big John came inside and squeezed into the tiny exam room. "Can we walk Bobby to the Jeep?" John asked.

"No, we'll need the sled," I decided. The last thing we need was for Bobby to collapse on the back steps. John ducked outside and returned with the orange transfer board. I cringed. Here we had a patient on a cardiac monitor, oxygen, and an IV, and the final transfer would be on an orange plastic sled. Mike padded the bed board as best he could and laid it on the floor. One more week and we'd have the used ambulance from the city, I sighed. One more week.

Bobby, for his part, was unperturbed. "I've slept on worse." John ran the restraining belts through the slots and loosely bound Bobby's feet and torso. He was about to snug up a third belt around his upper chest when I asked him to hold off; the risk was too high that it might slip and compress his neck. For good measure, Mike ran a continuous strip of duct tape around Bobby's lower chest, abdomen, and legs.

Lugging Bobby through the waiting room, we pushed open the front door and felt the sting of wet snow on our faces. Kathryn joined us outside, scowling as she threw a shovel and a set of tire chains onto the snow from the back of the Jeep. Overhead, two herring gulls flapped against the wind like mobiles, holding their position. Bobby waved and smiled. I followed his gaze. There, standing beside the upstairs curtain across the way, was Hazel, her thumb emphatically up.

"Any chest pressure or light-headedness?" I asked.

"None of that. Better off lying down though. You know, Hazel was quite a gal. Outgoing, not what I'd call a knockout, but she turned a few heads at the VFW mixers. Liked to dance, have a good time. Not wild, just fun. Thought she'd settle down with Clem Haskins, but it never happened."

"How long ago was that?" I asked. We were making the turn at the Down Front ice cream parlor, onto the cobblestones of Adam's Street. A blast of wind came up the hill and rocked the Jeep. I stuffed an extra blanket beneath Bobby's head.

"Fifteen, maybe twenty years ago, maybe longer. One day she was on the ferry or working at the store or dancing at the VFW, and the next thing I heard she was holed up in her house. Never come out since." The Jeep braked to a stop. The wind whistled off the roof of the freight shed.

"Think she'll ever leave the house?" I asked.

"If you ask me, she's waiting."

The tailgate released, and Big John, like a giant peering into a dark cave, flashed a nervous smile. "Fireboat's already tied up against the wharf, but she's taking an awful beating. They can't hold their position much longer." He looked at Mike. "This is going to be a bitch."

As we pulled the sled from the Jeep, Mike and I held one end while John, facing us, took the brunt of the gale. His wool cap flew off and spun across the wharf and out of sight.

"I need to ditch the oxygen tank," I yelled. "It's too unwieldy. We can't manage Bobby and hold onto the tank." I relaxed my hold on the stretcher and lifted the O2 cannula from Bobby's nose and rested the tank on a blanket back inside the Jeep.

When I returned, Mike and John discovered that they could more safely manage the transfer by laying the sled onto the wharf and pushing it forward with their boots. I hadn't noticed before, but Mike had wisely secured a rope to the sled while we'd been waiting at the health center and coiled it under the blanket.

Reaching the edge of the wharf, Mike cupped his hands over his mouth and called to the Medical Crisis Unit crew, "Raise your arms up. Let's see how far we need to go." Three pairs of arms lifted skyward; it would be another six feet.

I whispered in Bobby's ear, "Grasp the handrails as we lower you down. Remember, I don't want anyone touching your neck." Big John wrapped a double coil of rope around his fist and dug his feet into the base of an anchoring cleat as he belayed the sled off the dock face. Mike and I controlled the front rope to avoid a sudden flip of our cargo.

"Mike, we need to throw our lines to the crew," I shouted. "They can control the front of the sled from below." We threw our lines to the crew balancing on the rolling deck, their arms stretched upward into the whiteout. The slack was taken up, and John slowly played out more line.

Bobby Amundsen flashed an incongruous Cheshire cat grin as the sled disappeared over the edge.

A shout came from below, and the line went limp. I could see the crew, bent against the wind, carrying the stretcher into the pilothouse. The dock lines were released, and the fireboat churned into reverse, then groaned forward, sliding and creaking against the pilings, pointing toward the mainland.

We crowded into the front seat of the Jeep. Mike reminded me that the health center's oxygen tank was in the back. Big John said that tomorrow morning he and Mike would do something really fun—shovel out the fire hydrants on Island Avenue.

A few minutes later, I hung up my coat inside the health center. The clinic was empty. Kathryn was long gone. Wearily, I packed my stethoscope and scribbled a brief note on Bobby Amundsen. A cool draft swirled against my back. Better check the back door. I pulled out my pocket calendar: *HC Hazel?* Peering through the window I could see the pumpkin glow of a bedroom light across the way.

After straightening the waiting room chairs and tossing several stuffed animals into the toy bin, I locked the medication cabinet. In the rear of the clinic I opened the alarm box and activated the ten-second alarm, closed the box, switched off the waiting-room lights, and leaned against the back door, bracing for that first flush of arctic air. Rooted like an oak, the back door was wedged shut by ice and drifting snow.

I reared back and thumped heavily against the door jam. Nothing budged. *Woo-woo-woo!* The clinic alarm wailed. Fumbling in the dark I scraped my knuckles on the edge of the alarm box and shut the alarm down.

I checked the front door and pushed it open. From the alarm box to the front door was roughly thirty feet. I moved several waiting room chairs off to the side, zipped my parka, dimmed the lights, grabbed my bag, and pushed the red button. Then I sprinted through the waiting room and blew through the front door, pinwheeling across the porch, and crashed against the outside railing. On my hands and knees, I crawled across the landing and shut the clinic door. I held my breath. Silence.

Dusting myself off, I shuffled off the porch. Across the street I could see a shadowy form at the edge of the upstairs window. I raised a hand, and Hazel Towns waved back. She was expecting me, so I shuffled across the lane and let myself in.

CHAPTER TEN

The fishiest captain.

—Bud Perry

The ulcerated toe I'd diagnosed more than a year ago never healed. To his credit, Bud Perry wore white socks and kept the toe clean and dry, but there simply wasn't enough circulation to close the ulcer. Then Lisa stopped by one Saturday morning and found Bud delirious and combative, with a red streak extending from his foot up to mid-calf. I admitted him to the Osteopathic Hospital, where IV antibiotics pushed back the infection, but the toe required amputation. His kidneys failed, and dialysis was initiated at Maine Medical Center (as a small community hospital, the Osteopathic didn't have a dialysis unit). Somehow Bud Perry survived.

Discharged back to Peaks Island, Bud had settled into a new routine. At 5:45 a.m. on Mondays, Wednesdays, and Fridays, he tap-tapped his white cane from his apartment to the Gull for breakfast and coffee. At 6:45 he zipped up his parka, pulled on his mittens, and shuffled along the sidewalk past Feeney's Island Market, the post office, and Down Front before descending Welch Street for the 7:15 ferry. Commuters looked after him. If Welch Street was icy, someone invariably grabbed an arm and guided him down the hill to the boat.

A taxi met him on the Portland side and delivered him to Maine Medical Center, where he underwent three hours of dialysis. Then another taxi, another ferry, *tap-tap-tap* up Welch Street, a late lunch at the Gull, and an afternoon nap. This lasted two months.

Then another toe turned black. He was admitted to the Medical Center. A vascular surgeon consulted but decided Bud wasn't a candidate for revascularization. The major arteries were clogged and narrowed. The smaller arteries were clogged and narrowed. There was nothing healthy enough to bypass to. Bud figured they'd take the whole damn foot and be done with it, but, no, the doctors wanted to "save" the foot. Now it was another waiting game. Bud squinted at the hospital ID wristband next to his oversized digital wristwatch. The one-inch digital numbers were visible if he shut the left eye and held the watch to his nose: 6:00 a.m., time for another pain pill. He pushed the red call button.

The intercom above his bed crackled, "May I help you?"

"It's time for my pain pill."

"Your nurse will be right down."

His back ached. On Peaks he slept in a recliner. He wondered if Lisa could ship it across on the ferry, haul it through the lobby, and bring it up on the elevator. Maybe she could sneak him a bottle of whiskey. That would be nice. He felt for the phone and hesitated; a dim form walked into the room.

"Mister Perry?"

"Do you have my pain pill?"

"No, I'm Tom, the orderly. You've got a big day ahead of you. I'm here to take you to dialysis. With any luck you should be back here in your room before lunch. Are you able to slide out of bed and into the wheelchair?"

"I'm waiting for a pain pill. My foot is aching."

"They may need to take care of that in dialysis. Tight schedule today; if we don't get down and hook you up soon, everyone will be backed up."

"Well, I'm not everyone. I'm diabetic. I haven't eaten breakfast yet, and I need a pain pill." The orderly positioned the wheelchair next to the bed and set the brakes. Bud stiffened when he felt the firm hands behind his back but allowed himself to be brought to a seated position and held still as the orderly grasped his legs and swung them over the edge of the bed.

"Can you—"

"Get your paws off me. I can stand. Where's the wheelchair?" Bud could feel the blood rush to his feet and felt a tight, queasy sensation in the pit of his stomach. His foot like felt the end of the bed was resting on it. He eased himself down without a word. The orderly silently delivered him to the dialysis unit.

The dialysis nurse, Peggy, recognized him and took the wheelchair from the attendant, whispering in a sweet low voice, "What will it be today, Mister Perry—the bed or the recliner?" Off to his right, he could make out the dim outline of the cream-colored recliner and smiled inwardly; not so long ago, the offer would have triggered a double entendre—anywhere, anytime you're comfortable. But today he was relieved to ease into the recliner and pull his hat down before settling into a deep, dreamless sleep.

"Mister Perry, it's time; the attendant is here." It was Peggy. Bud cracked open an eye. A deep, boring pain in his foot flowed over him like hot ice. "We let you sleep; sometimes it's better that way." Bud nodded and shrugged. His tongue felt thick, and his lips were cracked and dry. Peggy pulled his hat off and ran a thick brush through his yellowed, matted hair before placing the hat back on. "They need to redress your foot. The blood soaked through the dressings. We held off on giving you your pain meds; the dialysis dropped your blood pressure down too low, and Doctor Himmelfarb worried you might bottom out with more meds. Oh, and be sure to tell your nurse; she needs to give you an early lunch. For some reason they didn't record any intake today, and your blood sugars are running low."

Bud sipped eagerly on the orange juice Peggy offered him and felt the fog recede. He knew by afternoon he'd feel better—not great, but better—and that was enough. He'd manage 'til then.

Back upstairs, the orderly jostled Bud's foot as he settled him into his bed. Bud wrapped his hand around the attendant's wrist. The attendant tried to pull his arm away, and Bud sensed the pain and doubt in the man's eyes. "Be gentle," Bud said slowly. "I've got a bad foot."

The orderly propped Bud's foot on a pillow and raised the head of the bed. Stepping back, he rubbed his wrist where Bud had grasped it and muttered, "Old bastard." And then he was gone—but not before knocking the call button onto the floor. Fresh blood flowed out from the edge of the dressing onto the bed sheet. Bud reached for the call button. Where was the damn call button? He reached over to the nightstand and groped for the phone, under a stack of magazines, behind the pillow—but there was no call button.

"Hey!" His voice cracked. He located the water pitcher and drank from it, spilling half down his gown. "Down here! I need some help!" he shouted. He'd asked—no, *insisted* on a private room, as far away from the chaos of the nursing station as possible. If it wasn't the endless chatter, it was some stiff going into cardiac arrest in the middle of the night or a new admission or the clang of oxygen tanks or some poor fool spewing gibberish over and over and over. No, he preferred it here, down at the end of the hallway. Alone.

"Hey! Anybody! Nurse? Nurse!" He slumped against the pillow and then suddenly reached over and slammed the bed stand against the wall, tipping the bedpan onto the linoleum. Urine flowed across the floor. "I need a nurse! Hey, anybody! *Help!*" His eyes narrowed, and he reached for the phone. He hesitated and slowly counted to ten and then placed the phone back in its cradle.

Cupping his hands around his mouth, he bellowed once more, *"I need a nurse, now!"*

Then he picked up the phone again. He dialed 911.

"Hello, Portland nine-one-one."

"I'm stuck in bed. I can't get up, and I have a foot that's bleeding out. I feel like I'm going to pass out. No food since last night. Urine everywhere."

"Calm down, calm down. You'll be okay. If you can, reach down and apply some pressure on the wound. That will stop the bleeding. Don't panic. We're on our way."

"Well, make it quick."

"What's your address?"

Bud smiled wickedly at the receiver. "I'm in room three ninety-three at Maine Medical Center. That's three-nine-three. *Now call my nurse!*"

Slamming the phone down, Bud puffed up his pillow and adjusted his cap. He clasped his fingers and cracked each knuckle and began to count. When he reached twenty-two, he heard the clamor of feet coming down the hallway. Angry feet.

Two nurses, an intern, a medical student, and a security guard burst into the room, all talking and yelling at once. Do you realize what you've done? Haven't you heard of a call button? Mr. Perry, 911 is for emergencies. You should be ashamed of yourself! Bud let them carry on for a few seconds before silencing them with a growl he reserved for special idiots.

"Now back off," he hissed. Their heads shot back like he'd thrown a glass of ice water in their faces. "First," he brought up a single finger and glared in their direction. "First, no food today. Nada. Nothing. Zero. It's 11:30, and I'm a diabetic. Get the picture? Second, no pain meds. Not even a Tylenol. Third, none of you clowns has been down since four this morning except when you woke me up to take my temperature. Anybody notice? I'm soaking the bed in blood. Anybody?" Against the far wall, the hospital staff stood, transfixed. "Fourth, the orderly dumped me back in bed without a call button. Fifth, nobody came when I yelled."

He paused, and the security guard started to break in. Bud ignored him. "Now, you know how loud I yelled? I yelled *this loud. Does everyone hear me now??* If I had a penknife, I'd take off this goddamn toe and be done with it. Now, you either pick up this mess, give me some grub, re-dress my foot, and treat my pain, or I'm calling nine-one-one again and transferring back to Peaks Island where I can at least get a drink. Now, get moving!"

The senior nurse whispered to her assistant, "I suggest we all get moving," and winked in Bud's direction. He couldn't see the wink, but there was nothing wrong with his hearing. Within moments, Bud could feel the pain slowly recede as a bolus of morphine infused into his subclavian line. He nibbled on a chicken sandwich while a nurse—the chubby, red-haired one he liked to tease—made cooing, clicking sounds like a sympathetic dove as she gently unwrapped his foot. She lied that the toe looked like it was coming along, but Bud didn't mind. He felt a warm flush as another bolus of morphine washed over him like a gentle spring tide, and he drifted off.

Later, when I stopped by, I noticed a yellow rose in a vase on the bed stand. A pillow was expertly positioned in the small of his back.

Bud's beard was brushed and trimmed. Bud wiggled his foot beneath the gauze and declared his foot was on the mend.

That spring, I signed up for a small boat course run by the Coast Guard. Not surprisingly, with life being what it is, I made it to exactly two sessions. Still, it was enough for Sandi to reluctantly agree to a boat. Not a year-round boat, but a runabout, a practice boat to explore the bay.

The classified ad read, *Boston Whaler, older boat, mint condition, 90 hp Mercury. Trailer works. $3,500.* The next Saturday I drove our truck onto the ferry and wiped the grime carefully off the ball on the trailer hitch. It read *2¼*. My friend Dave Quimby told me that most small boat trailers fit a two-inch ball, or maybe he said a 2¼–inch ball. How much difference can a quarter inch make? Suddenly, the image of my new used boat popping off the trailer ball and rushing down a hillside leaped to mind.

I pulled over to a phone booth and called the owner.

The phone rang for an uncomfortably long time. "Yeah?"

"Hello. This is the guy who's coming up this morning to look at your boat. We talked yesterday."

"What time is it?"

"It's 6:42."

"Listen, Mister 6:42, I've had a long night, and where I live, it's still dark. The sun won't come over the ridge for another hour, so if you don't mind—"

"I'm sorry, really, but I have a long drive ahead of me, and need to know if the boat trailer for the boat you're selling fits a two and a quarter- or two-inch ball. If I like the boat, I want to take it with me." Just saying that made me feel more knowledgable, more boat-worthy. More desperate.

"Have you got cash?"

"Well, no. But I'm prepared to write out a check today for the full amount, for the right boat. At the right price," I added.

Silence again. He coughed and cleared his throat. "No checks." I heard a pop and he sipped on something. A dog barked. "Your bank open today? If you can't bring cash, a bank check will have to do. Stop and get a bank check. Can you do that?"

I said I could.

"Two and a quarter-inch ball be fine."

Though spring was in full swing on the coast, it was still winter at Evans Notch, seventy miles inland. The calendar flowed backward as I drove due west into the mountains past leafed-out oaks and maples and bright fields of lupine. I was nearly by the gravel driveway when I braked and backed up. There, against an outbuilding, beneath four inches of corn snow, was my Boston Whaler. A broad-backed, stooped figure was visible at the bow, flinging scoopfuls of wet snow off the deck. A freshly opened can of Budweiser, balanced on the cowling of the engine, reflected first light coming off Speckled Mountain.

I cleared my throat. "Nice boat."

The man, Dave, rolled up his sleeves, exposing no less than twelve tattoos, and pulled out a garbage can from the shed, filling it with water until the propeller was submerged. He fired up the engine. Smoke billowed from the exhaust, and the lower unit rattled and shook, but I was impressed. Cold start, first time.

I squatted and took a look at the hull, looking for gouges or recent fiberglass work. One corner of the stern was cracked, but it was above the water line, and the wound looked superficial. Next to the crack was the logo: Sea-Whaler. I pulled out the classified ad and scanned the small print.

Dave looked up from his shoveling as if he could read my mind. "Paper made a mistake. I told them it was a Whaler, and they must've added the Boston on their own. The Sea-Whaler is a heck of a boat, maybe better than a Boston Whaler." Dave disappeared into the shed and came back with three life preservers, an oar, and a dinky mushroom anchor. "Divorce coming up in two weeks, and I need to get rid of my toys. The old lady's cleaning me out. What do you think?" he asked. I wanted the boat, but the divorce made me wary.

"How do I know she doesn't own the boat?"

"Just me on the title. Think I've got it inside somewhere." His voice had an edge to it. "Listen, you want the boat or not? I've got a friggin' headache, and this sun is killing me. Some other guy called and said he'd be down later this morning."

I wanted the boat, and yet . . .

"Mind if I write up an agreement?" I asked. Dave shrugged his shoulders and reached into the Whaler and pulled out another beer. I heard the groan of a motorcycle and looking up from my writing saw a low-slung Harley coming down the gravel road. Leaning the Harley on its kickstand, the newcomer, whose name was Jess, caught the unopened Budweiser Dave threw his way. His arms were massive enough to hold twice the tattoos Dave's did. Finishing up the agreement, I handed it to Dave, who handed it to Jess.

Jess reached into his back pocket where his wallet was connected by a chain to his front belt loop. He patted his front pockets. Then he reached up into his T-shirt pocket and found a tiny pair of granny glasses and rested them on the bridge of his nose. He turned his attention to the contract, but not before looking me over as if I were less than an insect. He handed the agreement back to Dave. Then Jess pulled off his glasses and in his best lawyerly voice said, "I think this will be satisfactory." I couldn't believe my ears. They weren't going to kill me. I handed over the money.

Back on the road, Bud Perry came to mind. It was a curious balance we'd reached. Bud liked the care and feel of the Osteopathic Hospital, but the Osteopathic Hospital didn't have a dialysis unit. For shorter admissions—say, a few weeks ago when he'd developed a raging kidney infection—I admitted him to the Osteopathic. For longer admissions he reluctantly agreed to admission at Maine Medical Center, where he could keep to his dialysis schedule.

In this case, Bud had been admitted to Maine Med under surgery. After a week of indecision, they'd finally amputated the second toe. He was too weak to come home, and the plan was to discharge him to the rehab facility to gain back some strength. I wondered if he might want to see my boat. It might lift his spirits. Pulling into Maine Med, luck was with me, and I parked just beyond the main entrance. Finding Bud wasn't difficult. He was propped up on a gurney next to the lobby elevator near the entrance. Beside him was a hospital orderly, a tall, stork-like man with shocks of peppery brown hair and a yellow cotton shirt buttoned to the neck. Bud's black and red wool mackinaw shirt hung loosely off his shoulders, and his head drooped forward, his chin nearly on his chest. On his lap was a plastic bag with his personal belongings.

His face was pasty and emotionless, like a schizophrenic on Thorazine. It was a shock to see Bud reduced to a shell of his former self. Had he given up?

The orderly craned his neck. "Any minute now, we'll get you across the street to the Rehab Hospital. Lot of people spend a few days, sometimes a week or two, getting back their strength at the Rehab. They push you, but they got to push you to get better. Here comes the ambulance now."

Bud lifted up his head. "What did you say?"

"I said, here comes the ambulance now. We'll have you on board and across the street in no time flat."

Bud pushed back the brim of his captain's hat. "Where's the ambulance going?"

The orderly gently patted Bud's shoulder and explained, "Don't worry, pops; we're just taking a ride across the street. Nothing to worry about."

"You mean, I'm getting into that ambulance so they can take me across the street to the Rehab?"

"Exactly." The orderly seemed relieved. Some old folks would get worked up when they saw the ambulance. It confused them. This old codger had more on the ball than most. "They're backing up. That way we can load up without you getting a chill."

"Who pays for this?"

"Medicare, I expect."

"It's a rip-off. I'm not getting in the ambulance. Wheel me across the street. I can see the front door from here," he lied.

The ambulance parked up against the entrance—immediately behind my Whaler—and two lanky attendants opened the rear doors. One of them held a clipboard and waved for the orderly to wheel Bud outside. The orderly waved them inside. "We got a problem; says he's not getting in the ambulance."

Bud sat up straighter on the gurney and reached into god knows where and found his pipe.

The attendant with the clipboard approached him, all business. "Mister Perry, its hospital policy. You're being discharged from one institution and admitted to another, and no one wants to see anything happen to you in between. It's for your own safety." He motioned for his partner to hold the door while he wheeled Bud through the doors.

"I know a rip-off when I see one," Bud's replied. "What are you getting from Medicare? Hundred fifty bucks for five minutes' work?" Bud's voice filled the foyer. The woman at the desk in admitting put her newspaper down and turned off the radio. "You people seem to think Medicare is some kind of lottery. I paid for Medicare, and I don't want my dough paying for a rip-off. Now wheel me across to the Rehab Hospital."

The attendant stood his ground. "Listen, you need to understand—"

"I don't need to understand anything," Bud cut him off. "You people are providing a service. It's a service I don't want and I don't need. Now get lost." At that moment, the elevator door opened, and a crisply dressed hospital representative arrived on the scene. Boy was that quick. I'd seen him in action before, and he seemed sincerely interested in patient care. Reasonable guy. Maybe he could wheel Bud across the street.

"Mister Perry." The hospital representative shook Bud's hand and patted his shoulder. "I'm Robert Ingraham, patient liaison. Now, what can I do for you today?"

"These knuckleheads don't understand the word *no*."

"Well, maybe I can help. Here's the situation. I know it must seem we're being overcautious, but it's hospital policy that we disallow private transfers between the two institutions. Please understand, this rule wasn't made to gouge Medicare; it's to ensure the gains you've made here aren't lost in a mishap."

I stepped forward. Enough was enough. These people didn't know who were dealing with. I'd wheel Bud myself across the street. But Bud was far from done. "What you're doing is committing Medicare fraud. It's illegal. It's a rip-off. Now call Regional Transportation."

"Excuse me?" The hospital liaison blinked.

"Regional Transportation. Seven-nine-nine, four-six-nine-one. Their job is to transfer the elderly and the disabled. It's publicly funded.

It's free. Medicare isn't ripped off, and they deal with cripples like me all day long." Out of the corner of his eye, the hospital liaison saw that traffic in the foyer had stopped. People were milling around, waiting, wondering what would happen next. Who was this man arguing with the sick old man on the stretcher? What was this about fraud?

"Mister Perry," the liaison struggled for the right platitude. "Mister Perry, we will give them a call," he exhaled, and motioned to the orderly. "John, call Regional Transportation. I'm sure the hospital has looked carefully into this, and we'll find Mister Perry's request is beyond the scope of their mission. Mister Perry, since the ambulance is here, I'm hoping you'll agree to—"

"They'll be right over." It was John, hanging up the phone. "Five minutes."

I stepped forward and extended a hand. "Rob Ingraham? I didn't recognize you for a minute. Doctor Radis. I take care of Mister Perry on Peaks Island. Good to see you. I'll wait here with Mister Perry until Regional arrives and get him tucked in at Rehab. The ambulance can be freed up for emergency calls." Rob suddenly remembered a meeting and, to his credit, said he'd learned a thing or two from Mr. Perry. The ambulance pulled away. I remembered the boat. "Say, Bud, you want to wait for Regional outside? I have something I want to show you."

I found a wheelchair against the far wall and helped Bud off the gurney. "Can you believe these knuckleheads?" Bud asked. He was clearly pleased with himself. I rolled him through the automatic doors and stopped in front of the Whaler.

"Well, well, well. You've finally got yourself a boat. What kind of engine?"

"Mercury, ninety horsepower, two stroke. It's only four years old. The motor, I mean." Bud wheeled himself to the stern and ran a hand over the metallic outlines of the engine, working his way down to the lower unit. I knew I'd gotten a great deal and told him so. "Only thirty-five hundred dollars. I'm heading from here to the public ramp and from there back to Peaks Island."

"Prop's bent."

"Meaning?"

"The guy rammed into something, bought a new propeller, but the lower unit's been damaged, and the prop is bent. You're going to get a lot of vibration, and that's going to tear apart the lower unit." He noticed the crack in the stern and ran a finger over the wound. "Probably when he did this. Fiberglass repair is piss-poor." He leaned forward and peered at the lettering, one letter at a time. "Sea-Whaler. You bought a lake boat, a Sea-Whaler. Keep your life preserver on; you hit a ledge, and this baby is going down like the *Titanic*, stern first."

"So . . . you like the boat," I joked. We both laughed.

"You could have done worse."

Regional Transportation pulled in. The van lowered an electric ramp. I joined Bud inside, and the driver shifted into first gear, braked, and came to a stop. Our journey took less than thirty seconds, time enough to take a sip of coffee, swallow, and say, "Thanks for the ride."

"Never been out here to Maine Med before," the driver said. "Some new program?"

Sandi, the plumber's assistant, thrived in her new job. Lately she'd been doing both plumbing and electrical work (her boss, Paul, was both a master plumber and a master electrician) and before bedtime happily recounted her day cleaning out clogged sewer lines, pulling wires, or repairing fuse boxes. There were two other women working for Paul part-time, no men. Paul liked the arrangement, claiming that women show up while men get the "flu" after a night of drinking at the Legion. He could be cranky and demanding, but Sandi and the other women just tuned most of that out. The job was physically difficult. They crawled under porches, sawed and sweated pipe, and stood or laid in half-frozen mud. On the days she worked, Sandi was so exhausted Paul would drop her off at our house at lunchtime for a thirty-minute nap.

Sandi's social work skills came in handy at her new job. She calmed down customers who were angry about delays. She helped Paul organize his schedule and improve his people skills. The three women were running the show.

It helped that Sandi had a low-maintenance ego. She didn't care much what people thought about her change in vocation. If anything, she underestimated her considerable abilities. This went back to her college field hockey days. Thirty-five years after graduation, a former teammate had said to her, "I went to the field hockey reunion last week. Isn't it amazing that after all these years you still hold the single season and career records for assists at Bates?"

Sandi had said, "What record?"

Molly went everywhere with us in a backpack. She was a happy, mellow baby. Just wait, Sandi's mom Jean had said; mellow babies could suddenly transform into difficult babies. "Enjoy her now. It may not last." In the back of my mind I worried that Molly would suffer a learning disability associated with her difficult birth. The image of her limp, blue body immediately after birth still haunted me. It helped that Sandi wasn't worried—not one bit.

Kate loved part-time daycare but—surprise!—was prone to losing any- and everything. Sandi and I attended the daycare open house and Angie, Kate's teacher, said that before Sandi left she should check the lost and found box. Good idea. With fourteen children in daycare, Kate's lost items accounted for three-quarters of the box's contents. "How'd this get in here," I asked Angie, plucking my favorite knit cap from beneath Kate's mittens.

Hazel Towns and I had struck up a friendship since I visited her during the prior winter's blizzard. For her part, she held her tongue at the sight of my bloody hand (where I'd scraped it on the alarm box escaping the health center). The first time I examined her she'd been nearly unable to rise from a chair; her hair coarse and visibly thinned, her lower legs puffy and sallow. Yet her sense of humor remained intact. No, more than that. Her humor had been *weird*. She'd seemed completely oblivious to her disabilities. On a hunch, I pulled out my reflex hammer from my bag and assessed her reflexes. I'd never before observed "hung-up" reflexes—a slowing of the relaxation phase when a reflex hammer triggers a reaction in a tendon—but there it was: the Achilles tendon took its good, sweet time returning to the neutral position. Hypothyroidism.

When her thyroid hormone level came back nearly undetectable, I'd prescribed a thyroid-replacement pill. Over the next several months Hazel regained her muscle tone and dropped twenty pounds. I was sorry to see the myxedematous wit go.

Hazel dreamed that she might someday walk out the front door, cross the street, and come in for an office visit. That would be something. Twelve years in her house, she declared, was long enough. It was time to get out and stretch her legs and walk over to Feeney's Market or to church or maybe ride the ferry to town.

One morning at the clinic, I watched Hazel open the doorway across the lane and wave in my direction before tipping a dustpan into the rose bush. The door closed. People wondered about Hazel. The clerk at Feeney's claimed Hazel was simply a recluse—some folks just want to be left alone. But that just wasn't true of Hazel. She loved nothing more than to gab on the phone or welcome visitors with homemade pie and fresh lemonade.

I wondered sometimes if there had been a triggering event, a lost lover or death of a child, but when I probed deeper into her personal life, Hazel abruptly changed the subject. One day I said that medications made it easier for people with agoraphobia to work through their fears, but she stiffened and said she wanted to remember those fears; the last thing she wanted was to forget. Tranquilizers were for crazy people, she said. She'd leave her house when she was ready. "You'll see."

Ricky Hogan was on the ferry with his mother and older brother. At thirteen, he'd shot up several inches since winter, but his shoulders remained slumped, his face gaunt and expressionless. At the cuff of his windbreaker a fresh wrapping of gauze around his wrist told me all I need to know.

Mrs. Hogan fell in with me as we converged on the stairway leading down to the gangplank while Ricky hung back with his brother. "At least he's home for the weekend. That's something," she said, shaking her head. "Now the therapist wants to blame his lack of progress on someone, so she called a family meeting and wanted to know if there was anything I wanted to tell her. Tell her? Like *I'm* the problem? Then she leaned over toward me, like she's Perry Mason, private eye, and said, 'Mrs. Hogan, there has to be a reason Ricky has refractory anorexia and keeps cutting himself. We think there might be something more, something in the family dynamic, some type of secret Ricky hasn't shared with us that's keeping him sick.' Like I'm the monster. Like Ricky's sickness is all my fault. Bunch of crock."

I chose my words carefully. "Mrs. Hogan, everybody's frustrated. We all want Ricky to get better. Even therapists can get off on the wrong track sometimes."

Behind us Kate squirmed off of Sandi's lap and caught Ricky on the stairway. She reached up and unexpectedly grabbed his hand and explained that to cross the gangplank she needed to hold a big person's hand. That was the rule. For a moment, a wistful smile spread across Ricky's face. Before he could mouth the word *no*, Kate led the way across the gangplank. Releasing his hand, she skipped ahead and clambered up onto the stone wall. With his free hand, Ricky applied pressure where a trickle of blood dribbled down his wrist. Then his shoulders slumped, and his head drooped forward. He shuffled up the hill.

CHAPTER ELEVEN

As physicians, we should strive to cure a few, help most,
but comfort all.

—William Osler, MD

My boat lasted four months. Then it sank. Those four months
I learned a lot about boats, but not enough to prevent it
from sinking. The actual sinking was nothing special; a
drenching gale roared up the coast in November packing a one-two
punch—five inches of rain followed by forty-five-mile-an-hour gusts.
The rain turned to sleet, the sleet to snow. *SAKAMO*—named for
Sandi, Kate, and Molly—lurched up and down on her mooring, water
sloshing from front to back. One moment *SAKAMO* was afloat, and
then a wave broke over the bow, and she headed for the bottom.

The sinking was judged by those in the know (which apparently
included everyone on the island except me) so overdue, so inevitable,
that the actual sinking was acknowledged as if it had happened weeks
before. On my way to the clinic, I stopped by Feeney's Market. Mr.
Feeney said that after the rain and snow it was good to see the sun. "The
wind's backed off. Going to be a warm day, but that's November for
you." He was sorry to hear about my boat and asked if there were any
other boats nearby still on their moorings. Come to think of it, I admitted, *SAKAMO* was the only one.

"The other boats, they were pulled some time ago," he said, par-
roting back my words like a good therapist. He raised one eyebrow,
waiting. He would later say, "I could see it in his eyes; there was no
connection. When it comes to boats, the man is dumber than a hake."

I looked at my watch. "Well, I've got to go; health center opens
soon."

Bud Perry sat behind a card table in a folding chair in front of Feeney's in his bulky plum winter parka smoking his pipe. On the table were packages of light bulbs. I thought about avoiding Bud by going up Luther Street but decided instead to quietly sneak by.

"Heard *SANKA* sank." For a guy who was legally blind, Bud saw most everything that interested him. He pointed to the energy-efficient light bulbs. "Lion's Club is supporting the Boy Scout troop on the Island. Don't be a cheap sh—t; buy some bulbs." I reached into my back pocket. Shoot—no wallet. Now, how did that happen? I knew I'd had my wallet when I'd emptied out my pockets the night before, before bed. Luckily, in my front pocket was a five-dollar bill. I handed it over to Bud and stashed the package of three light bulbs in my backpack—where my wallet lay on top of a medical journal.

"If you flush out the engine with freshwater as soon as you pull your boat, you might avoid a total loss." Bud pulled the pipe from his mouth and flashed a gap-toothed smile. "Did I ever tell you the difference between a Sea-Whaler and a Boston Whaler?"

I glared at him and tried to think of something clever, some biting retort, but all that came out was, "Don't be late for your appointment. And bring your damn foot with you."

"If it's totaled, don't wait too long before you get another boat," Bud called after me. "You haven't lived out here long enough if you haven't sunk a boat. Remember that."

At the steps of the health center I cracked my neck to the right and left to clear my head. Before opening the door, I stole a look across the way, and, sure enough, there was Hazel Towns, peeking through her upstairs window. I wiggled a finger her way, as if to say, *I know you're spying on me.*

Bobby Amundsen was my first patient. Before his pacemaker, I hadn't known the man; he and I occupied the same island but traveled in parallel universes. Now I saw him everywhere. There was Bobby down at the wharf or drinking coffee at the Gull or dropping off an old sofa at the dump. The day before I'd noticed him sitting with Bud on the stone wall. We had a connection now. When he passed me in his truck, he'd lift his index finger off the steering wheel and I, in turn, would lift my finger, and nod in subtle recognition.

Bobby is on a statin medication for his high cholesterol. His pacemaker is working as intended. It is a successful lobster season and, over the course of two weeks, Bobby had pulled sixty traps at a time, backing up his truck to a finger pier and delivering the traps to his barn off Pleasant Avenue. Tucked inside each of his 720 traps are two bricks for ballast, an orange bait bag, sixty feet of line, and his signature red, white, and green buoys. Over the winter he will repaint the buoys, change out frayed lines, and replace traps too banged up to fish another season.

Some lobstermen fish through the winter, but it's a deeper water fishery. As Casco Bay cools off, lobsters move from the shallows surrounding the inner islands to open deeper water—the fall crawl. The risk goes up exponentially; even the largest boats wallow in the deep swells. The deep-water fishery is a young man's game.

A few weeks before *SAKAMO*'s demise, Bobby spent the better part of a Saturday putting his lobster boat up. At low tide he'd driven his pickup onto the beach and attached a cable from the rear bumper to the front end of the cradle where it was stored above the high-tide mark. Then he lugged four heavy planks out of the brush and placed them beneath the cradle. Back in the truck he dragged the cradle the length of the planks, gotten out of his truck, and yelled, "Hey, Doc! Tide's turned; I don't have all day to get this cradle in place. Why don't you stop gawking and give me a hand?"

"Who, me?" I said, leaning against the railing of the wharf, sipping a cup of coffee. "Sure."

I picked my way down to the beach, the wet snow working its way into my boots. From behind the cradle, I grasped a plank and dragged it to the front, refashioning the plank roadway. Bobby stayed in the truck and put it in gear, towing the cradle another ten feet toward the incoming tide. When the cradle was in position, Bobby disconnected the cable from the truck and reattached it to the rear of the cradle. Then I attached a winch to the free end of the cable and dragged the business end up the hill and wound it around a weathered oak.

"Doc, that'll do for now." Bobby then climbed back into his truck. "Come back at two, when the tide's washed over the cradle. And bring a pair of waterproof boots. Once we have the *Ruth Anne* onto the cradle, we're in business. Before you go, can you stack a few stones onto the cradle bed? I'd do it myself," he winked, "but I'm under a doctor's care."

When I returned, Bobby was already aboard the *Ruth Anne*, his dinghy trailing off the stern. He guided the boat onto the cradle, secured the lines, and scrambled onto the foredeck to attach the bowline. Then he climbed into the dinghy and paddled around the vessel, making minute adjustments by poking the stern with his paddle. I noticed he wasn't wearing a life preserver. Chances are, I thought to myself, Bobby doesn't know how to swim.

As the tide receded, the *Ruth Anne* settled nicely onto her winter resting place, and Bobby joined me ashore. "See if you can engage the winch; sometimes it can be a bit cranky." I waded through the snow up to the birch and realized I hadn't a clue how to make a winch work. Bobby joined me and patiently reviewed the basics of winch winding. We changed places, and I returned to more familiar work, plank placement, and the *Ruth Anne* inched up the beach until she was safely stored above the high-tide mark.

Only then had it occurred to me: Bobby usually did this job himself.

We sat on upside-down bailing pails and watched the sun set over House Island, the light reflecting off the windows of the solitary house on the point. Bobby wondered how much longer he'd be welcome to store his boat on the beach. Maybe he'd be pushed off by a sailboat or cruiser if some summer person squawked loud enough. He asked if I'd noticed the new stop sign on Pleasant Avenue or the huge foundation Donny Gregor had poured last fall on the backshore. "Got to be a monster of a house for a foundation like that. Watched him bulldoze a perfectly good cottage to make room for the footings." He'd skipped a rock into the water and stood and stretched. "Good to have that done. Thanks."

One January morning, in the midst of the biggest snowstorm of the season, Johanna von Tiling slipped off her toilet and fractured her hip. The answering service relayed her number to me on my beeper. Her friend Chester Pettengill was at the house and put her on the line. "Doctor

Radis, somehow I've fallen. I'm concerned that I've broken my hip. The emergency people are here at the house and have me on a stretcher."

I worried. Even if Johanna survived the surgery, many elderly patients who fracture a hip don't survive beyond six months. At the very least, it was unlikely that she'd return to her home on Cliff Island. "Stop right where you are!" Johanna ordered. "Don't you people know the first thing about immobilization of a possible hip fracture? Doctor Radis, are you still there?"

"Yes, Johanna, I'm still here."

"You know my case better than anyone. I've decided that I want you to be my attending physician at the Osteopathic Hospital."

I must admit, I didn't answer right off. There was a part of me, motivated by self-preservation, that wanted to simply say no. From that moment on, I knew that every order—from stool softeners to my choice for a surgeon to medication orders—would be scrutinized and second-guessed. On the other hand, it was possible she *could* be less ornery, less combative, less imperious. "Okay, Johanna. When you come off the rescue boat in Portland, tell the ambulance driver to take you to the Osteopathic Hospital. We'll get an X-ray and have one of the orthopedic surgeons see you. In the meantime—"

"Doctor Radis, I know full well the dangers of unnecessary radiation from X-rays. I would much prefer having a consultation with a surgeon, and if he deems it necessary, we can proceed to a radiograph. An X-ray may be totally unnecessary. What is the name of the surgeon?"

I closed my eyes and said, "Doctor John Bludgeon."

"John Bludgeon? The man sounds like a butcher."

I bit my lip. "Johanna? I think we're losing our connection. We'll figure this out when you arrive in the emergency room." I placed the telephone gently back onto the receiver. It was nearly dawn. Off the beach, a pair of eiders maintained their position just behind the shore break, diving for mussels as the snow fell in misty sheets across the bay. Sandi padded down the stairs in her slippers and bathrobe. She held Molly against her chest and poured herself a bowl of bourra.

"Snow day?"

"They're taking Johanna off Cliff Island in the fireboat. She probably broke a hip last night. I need to go and get her settled in at the

Osteopathic. I don't know how long it will take. If I take the next ferry, I'll have time to catch up on medical records at the hospital and maybe make an early ferry home this afternoon."

I called John Bludgeon, and he agreed to meet Johanna when she arrived in the ER. If anyone could talk over Johanna, I decided, it was John. He would pretend to listen to Johanna's concerns and then do exactly what he thought was appropriate. I liked the idea that John would make first contact with Johanna. My role was to manage her through any medical complications until discharge to . . . where? A nursing home? A rehab facility? That was where it would get dicey.

When I arrived at the emergency room, John stood at the X-ray view box, the soft white light reflecting off his bald head. Johanna's fracture was visible from across the room; the femur was splintered close to the femoral head, and there was considerable shortening and angulation. John pulled on the end of his mustache and seemed to lick his lips in anticipation. If there were ever a man born to cut, it was John Bludgeon. I liked John because he was meticulous in the OR and decisive when a patient needed surgery but completely deferential when it came to the nuances of internal medicine. "I hope you don't mind, but I gave her a shot of Demerol when she came in the door," he said. "Enough to take the edge off."

"Has she signed the permit?" I asked.

"No problem. I showed her the films and told her without surgery she'd die." John scribbled Johanna's name on an index card. "Her preop lab should be back in another fifteen minutes; then we'll take her upstairs. The sooner we fix this hip the better."

I found Johanna in a holding room, her right hip stabilized with sand bags and an IV infusing into her forearm. She looked pale and contracted, more like a fragile old woman than the feisty Cliff Islander I'd come to know and fear.

"Johanna." I tapped her arm. "Johanna."

She opened her eyes and looked dully around. I scanned her med sheet and noted the dose of Demerol she'd received: seventy-five milligrams. Not unreasonable for a hip fracture but enough, in her case, to completely snow her. Well, thank goodness for pain meds. I scanned her EKG, and nursing handed me her pre-op labs. Both were rock solid. I wrote an order to reduce the rate of her IV fluids and adjusted her oxygen rate. "You're going to do just fine, Johanna."

Her eyes flickered open again, and she struggled to recognize me. "Doctor Radis," she slurred, "this Doctor Butcher, is he a bludgeon? Is he a bludgeon?" she repeated, and her eyes drooped shut. A nurse opened the curtain and informed me they were ready upstairs. She wheeled Johanna across the hall to an open elevator.

I imagined the anesthesiologist giving Johanna a dose of Seconal before tilting her head back and sliding an endotracheal tube into her windpipe. Doctor Bludgeon would help the OR staff position Johanna on her side, fracture side up, with a foam block holding her legs slightly apart. Then he'd scrub his hands methodically for five minutes before returning to the operating room to gown and glove.

He'd hang back, watching the staff apply a liquid disinfectant to the hip and would hold up two fingers, indicating the need for a second application for good measure. A sterile drape would come next, obscuring everything except the surgical site. Only then would he approach the hip and in a long, flowing incision expose the tensor fasciae latae overlying the trochanteric prominence, suctioning and cauterizing as he went. Johanna's resilience, her blustery uniqueness, would be reduced to a side note—or nearly so.

I was told later that Dr. Bludgeon looked up from his work and pointed the scalpel at the operating room team. "Doctor Radis says this lady, Johanna von Tiling, is the queen of Casco Bay. We're dealing with royalty here, so keep sharp. If there's a slipup, there'll be hell to pay."

I caught the 12:45 ferry home and spent the afternoon sledding with Kate and Sandi at Tolman Heights, at sixty-eight feet the highest point on Peaks Island. Molly, now nearly a year old, squealed as Sandi and I clutched her to our chests on the lower slope. Kate came screaming down from the higher crossroads and slid nearly to the backshore. On the way home, I pulled the truck over at the Ice Pond and reached into the back seat and pulled out our skates. As darkness descended, a crescent moon peaked over the bay, the shadow skirting Cliff Island on the horizon. Bobby Amundsen sat on the edge of the pond and fed the warming fire. Sandi and I took turns skating with Kate while the other held Molly.

The following Thursday morning, an off day for dialysis, Bud Perry settled into his table at Lisa's, sipping black coffee. I looked at my watch and pulled up a chair. Bud never looked well, but today he looked worse than usual. I noticed the swelling around his ankles and wondered if he was in heart failure. He swirled the remnants of his coffee around. Lisa saw the motion from the counter and came by to fill his cup. Bud placed his hand over the top and waved her off.

"No, I've had enough. Thanks." It was the only time I'd heard him use the word. "Doc, we've got a problem on this island, and I think you should know about it." I could barely make out his voice and leaned in closer. "Seems like the Hogan boy, Ricky, was raped last year, probably on a camping trip with the Boy Scouts out on Picnic Point."

"Rape?" I pushed my pastry off to the side. "Are you sure?"

Bud winced as he shifted his leg under the table. "His mom and brother go up to visit him at the Augusta mental health facility a couple of days ago. Ricky's, like, gorked out. Ever since he tried to jump off the ferry when he was home on a weekend pass last month, they've got him doped up. Anyway, his mom and brother slip down to the lunchroom while Ricky's napping. Eventually they leave. In the car, his brother feels something in his coat pocket. It's a letter from Ricky—probably wrote it before he tried to jump off the *Machigonne* and stashed it in his brother's coat when they were out of the room."

"Did he mention who did it?"

"He did." Bud took the pipe from his mouth and pointed toward the kitchen. "I can hear him in there—Tommy Reynolds. Started up the scout troop on Peaks a couple of years ago. The guy is a first-class scumbag." I leaned back in my chair, and framed in the entrance to the kitchen was Tommy. His gray hair was trimmed short with a bald spot at the top where the skin was reddened and peeled. At the top of his T-shirt a tuft of chest hair billowed up from the nape of his neck. I recognized him; he'd visited the clinic last year to refill a prescription for his psoriasis; certainly not a very friendly guy, but rape?

"Are you sure?" I asked.

"I am." Bud's eyes half-closed. His head drooped heavily against his chest.

"Then what's he doing here?" I could hear my voice rising. "Aren't the police going to arrest him?"

"His mom went to the police this morning and asked me to sit in on the meeting." Bud's voice was no more than a whisper. "It doesn't look good. It happened more than a year ago. There's no physical evidence. No witnesses. Ricky's been in and out of the lockdown unit at the state mental hospital in Augusta."

"But they could still take it to trial, couldn't they?"

"Possibly. The police say it's basically his word against Tommy Reynolds's, and if it comes down to putting him on the witness stand . . ." Bud looked away. "Thing is, a trial could be good for him, or it could be bad."

"Do many people know?"

"The police, a few others. But news has a habit of spreading on this island. More than likely, people will wait a few days and see what the police are going to do."

"And then?"

Bud raised his coffee cup. This time, when Lisa came over, he placed the cup back on the table and watched her fill it halfway before whispering in her ear. She scowled at him but returned with a shot glass filled with an amber fluid. Bud stared out over the bay and sipped his coffee slowly before downing the shot.

"Clinic open today?" he asked. I nodded silently. Bud carefully placed the shot glass back on the table. His hand was shaking. "I'll see you later this morning. I think I'm dying."

Outside the health center, the nuns' Nissan van was parked neatly next to the clinic ramp. I chalked this up to pure chance and proceeded inside. Sister Mia waited her turn next to a little boy with a croupy cough seated on his mother's lap. Sister Mia asked the boy if he'd washed his hands that morning. When he said yes, Sister Mia suggested he do so again, now.

It was Sister Marie Henry's turn first. Stooped and bent from spinal osteoporosis, she quietly took a seat in the exam room. I explained to her that we were going to try something new—synthetic calcitonin, a new treatment for osteoporosis. As I drew up Sister Marie Henry's calcitonin, a vision of Ricky flashed in my mind. He was emaciated and clasping his knees to his chest, his eyes hollow and unseeing. Without warning, I dropped the vial, the glass shattering on the floor. I found the whisk broom beneath the sink and swept up the mess. Sister Marie Henry looked at me quizzically but rolled up her sleeve while I drew up another dose of calcitonin.

Across the hallway, Sister Mia was pacing. "We are blessed with Ricky's breakthrough. The truth and God's love will give him the strength he needs." She wiped her palms on her skirt and sat down, resting her pocketbook on her lap, waiting for me to speak.

"Sister Mia," I chose my words carefully, mindful that she may or may not know the full story. But what was the full story? Had there been a rape, or was this the tortured machinations of a young man's mental illness? "Have you spoken with Ricky recently?"

Without warning, Sister Mia slapped her palm on the counter, rattling the shelf. "In God's name, this evilness shall not go unpunished! He was only a child . . ." Her face sagged. She dabbed her eyes with the edge of her exam robe. "Have you spoken with Mister Perry?"

In the background I could hear the chatter of the waiting room and the opening and closing of the refrigerator in the lab. Framed by the window, two gulls circled above the building before settling onto the peak of Hazel Towns's house. Below them, a snowblower whirred, and a teenage boy, home from school on the snow day, shoveled the porch.

I turned to Sister Mia, and my eyes settled on her neck where her carotid arteries pulsed ominously. Every action has a reaction. Ricky's illness, like a pebble dropped into a still pond, had spread ever outward, threatening to take Sister Mia in its wake. Finally, I said, "I found out this morning. How long have you known about the rape?" There, it was out in the open.

"Mister Perry informed me. Prior to this, I have had my suspicion there was more to this than we knew. The man in question has been a suspect in a number of criminal acts in the community. As for Ricky, he has not, as yet, unburdened himself to me."

"You mean the only way we know the rape occurred is in a note he sent home in his brother's jacket?" I asked.

"No, Doctor Radis," Sister's Mia's voice sharpened. "We know a rape occurred because it is the only explanation for this poor child's fall from health. I believe him with all my heart and with all of God's love. Already he grows stronger. I can feel this. His healing has already begun."

I wanted to believe in Ricky; I wanted him to recover, but my training held me back from making a final judgment. Taking Ricky's claims at face value was easy for Sister Mia—her entire life was based on faith. But if I was to play a role in restoring Ricky's health, did I need the same unshakable faith?

Something about Sister Mia's words worried me. Wasn't it when Polly had finally been able to admit her depression and seemed to be making progress that she was most fragile? She had been seeing a counselor. She had been getting stronger. And then she hung herself. I had missed, perhaps, an opportunity to intervene, lulled into the belief she was on the mend.

Sister Mia stood abruptly and said it was time to go. "If I stay much longer, your assistant will take my blood pressure, and I am not under the delusion it will be satisfactory. I will go home and pray for Ricky's recovery. You have other patients to attend to. Mister Perry, I believe, is in need of your attention across the hall."

There was, in fact, a distracting, pungent, fruity odor in the air.

Outside Bud's room, the thick, heavy scent of tobacco smoke undercut the mysterious smell, and I knew Bud was smoking his pipe. Inside, even more surprising, Kathryn ignored this transgression as she silently unrolled a filthy ace wrap from his calf. Bud chewed on his pipe and grunted slightly as she pulled the last of the bandage from his skin. Depositing the dripping mess into the receptacle, she double wrapped the plastic bag and took it outside to the trash. I bent down for a closer look and knew we were in trouble. The wound was deep, and the edges were liquefying where the infection had eroded the subcutaneous tissues. On one edge, the pink ropy edge of Bud's calf muscle was visible.

I probed the wound with a Culturette and smelled the swab. It smelled vaguely like applejack. *Pseudomonas aeruginosa.*

"I caught my leg on the edge of my La-Z-Boy sometime last week," Bud said. "Some of the hardware must have worked loose on the foot rest, and I could feel the skin tear when I brushed against it. This morning, I feel like crap. How bad is it?"

I swallowed. "Bad enough that we need to hospitalize you and treat it with a combination of intravenous antibiotics. Even then—"

"Do what you can here." His voice trailed off. "No more hospitals."

"Bud, you're due for dialysis tomorrow."

"No more dialysis."

"We'll get you started on antibiotics at the hospital and see about getting you home by Saturday." I knew I was being overly optimistic. *Pseudomonas aeruginosa* is often a fatal infection, particularly in diabetics, particularly in diabetics with poor circulation and renal failure. In all likelihood he would lose the leg—or worse. Even now the infection may have reached his bloodstream and seeded his artificial heart valve. Bud shivered and nearly dropped his pipe.

"I've made up my mind."

"Bud . . ."

He closed his eyes and seemed to be drifting off again. He shivered again and drew himself up. "I have a few things to put in order, a few requests." He took a deep draw on his pipe, and it seemed to revive him. Smoke swirled around his head. "First. This is the last time I can make it to the clinic. I'll walk home." I looked at him dubiously. "I'll walk home, but I need you to treat me there from now on. Can you do that?"

"I can do that," I answered.

"Second, if I lose consciousness, I want to die on the island. You do nothing unless I say it's okay. I know my rights. You can't make me accept treatment I don't want. Is that clear? Kathryn?"

"Yes," Kathryn answered from the reception desk. "You're very clear."

"Do you understand me, Doc?"

"Yes, Bud, I understand."

"In fact, I forbid you to transfer me, and Kathryn is a witness. You transfer me to the hospital and cut off my leg, and I sue your ass off. Don't think I won't do it. Third . . ." at this, Bud's voice dropped to a whisper. "I want you to scatter my ashes in Hussey Sound. Orrin, my brother, knows that, but he's going to be shook up about this, and I don't have it written down. I want you to make sure it happens. I want them scattered in the Hussey. Can you do that for me?"

"I'll do that for you, Bud," I answered.

"Good. Then let's get going. Give me a shot."

I dressed the wound with Silvadene ointment and gave Bud a shot of the antibiotic ceftriaxone. It would have to do until the cultures returned. With luck, maybe the wound would grow out a sensitive staph or strep. I wasn't about to give up. Bud wouldn't be the first patient to stop dialysis only to rethink the decision when an infection cleared. When I finished wrapping the wound, Bud shuffled to the checkout window and settled his bill.

The next day I followed up with Bud at his apartment across from the Gull. I unwrapped the bandages and cleaned and debrided the ulcer. Bud sat in his La-Z-Boy recliner, his leg propped up on two pillows, the radio tuned to Maine Public Radio. He informed me that I was late. I noticed someone had duct-taped the edges of the footrest where the metal hinge had scraped his calf. Lisa came by with a sandwich and rinsed Bud's dishes and emptied the urinal he kept beside the recliner.

On the second day I brought Kate. Molly was perched in my backpack. It was after dinner, and I'd told Sandi she needed to get out of the house and take a walk. Kate immediately noticed the collection of pipes scattered on the kitchen table. "Daddy, we could make a toy house with these."

"Then I'll huff and I'll puff and I'll blow the house down," Bud growled.

"Do the pig noise!" Kate begged. A series of barnyard oinks and barks, moos and neighs, filled the air. "Again! Do the pig noise!" Kate held the edge of her yellow blankie to her cheek and giggled with delight. I crouched down and, shielding her view of Bud's leg, unwound the gauze and lifted off the Telfa Dressing. I choked back a cough and held my breath; the wound was expanding, and the sweet, fruity smell of *pseudomonas* flooded the room. His foot below the wound was dark and cold.

"Kate, can you get the coloring book from your knapsack and draw Mister Perry a picture?" I placed Molly on the floor with her. "And see if Molly can hold a crayon and make a line on the paper. Can you do that?"

Kate located the crayons and sat down on the rug beneath the picture window and went to work. I applied a thick coating of Silvadene to the wound and rewrapped the leg. "Bud," I whispered, "I really need to treat this in the hospital. Let me call the fireboat. The antibiotic I'm giving you isn't adequate; you need a combination of intravenous antibiotics and a surgeon to debride the ulcer. We need to do this now."

"No. I'm going to play this out. I'm not having much pain. Only time I've been thankful for the neuropathy. Your daughters made my day. We'll see you tomorrow." He lifted his cap and ran a hand through his hair before reaching for his pipe. His hand trembled, and he couldn't pack the bowl, much less light the pipe. I took the pipe from his hand and filled it for him. Bud reached over and grasped my wrist. "Pick out a pipe. Take the rest of the pouch; it wouldn't hurt you to smoke a bowl now and then."

Kate gathered up her crayons and handed me her picture of a red boat to give to Bud. Below the waterline were Molly's blue scratch marks. Kate stayed her distance, waiting quietly by the door. I picked up Molly and placed her in the backpack. She was asleep. As we opened the door, three island men dressed in scruffy jeans and fishing boots came up the walkway. One I knew from the marina, another, I thought, plowed roads for the city in the winter. Bobby Amundsen nodded sullenly. He pinched his cigarette out and crushed it with his heel before entering Bud's home.

"Daddy, were those bad men?" Kate asked as we walked along Island Avenue.

"No," I answered, half lost in thought, turning over my medical options, debating whether I should call the fireboat and, what? Force Bud on board? The MEDCU people would never go along with it anyway. Bud was right; people can't be forced to get the medical care they need. In all likelihood, hospitalizing Bud at this point wouldn't make a difference anyway. His time was drawing short. "No, they're not bad men. They're worried about Bud, and that makes them look serious."

"Daddy, Bud looked sick." She leaned her head against my side. "Is he getting the right medicine?"

CHAPTER TWELVE

Pain is inevitable; suffering is optional.

—Unknown

After midnight, four men left their homes and slowly walked along a dirt road deeper into the island's interior. In front of a two-story shingled cottage, they stood in the shadows, listening. A pickup moved slowly toward the group. It ground to a stop, and a lanky figure emerged and grabbed a ladder and a pair of wire cutters from the truck bed. Snow crackled under his boots.

Leaning the ladder against the house, Bobby Amundsen put on a pair of rubber gloves and silently climbed the ladder. With a snap, the electrical cable fell away from the house and recoiled like an angry snake as it hit the ground. The group emerged from the shadows and filed silently into the house.

Bobby flicked on a flashlight and sat down at the kitchen table. Footsteps paced back and forth directly overhead. "I'd stay upstairs where you are, Tommy," Bobby called out. "We've some work to do down here." Then he reached over and tore the phone from the wall, flinging it up the stairs. The pacing stopped. "Tommy, sit down on your bed and wait."

The islanders set to work, methodically ripping off anything that hung from the walls—paintings, built-in cabinets, stereo speakers—before attacking the sheetrock and trim boards with crowbars and hammers. Chairs were flung out the rear window, followed by the kitchen table, a sofa, and a desk, papers and bills scattering in the wind. The sink and toilet were pulverized with sledgehammers, the upright piano reduced to fragments no larger than a shoebox. As an afterthought, Bobby loosened a beam separating the kitchen from the living room

177

and, hanging on one end, sent it crashing to the floor. As one, the islanders picked up the beam and thrust it into the ceiling, sending it through the upstairs floor like an oversized dagger.

Bobby shouted upstairs. "Tommy, I know you can hear me, so listen up. We want you on the 6:15 morning ferry to Portland. You wore out your welcome on Peaks Island a long time ago. Don't bother contacting the police. No witnesses. No fingerprints. It's not likely there'll be much interest in solving this case. Watch your back, Tommy."

They climbed into the bed of the pickup and continued down the dirt road to the open ocean, where they collected driftwood for a fire and changed into clean clothes from the pickup. The bonfire consumed the clothing, even as the tide moved higher up the beach. In an hour, the sea extinguished the flames, the ash and debris drifting with the ingoing tide toward Hussey Sound.

Just before dawn, I woke in a sweat and wondered if Bud was dead. Lisa had said she'd stay with him until midnight, but she needed to get up early and open her coffee shop. The pace of his infection had quickened, and I knew it couldn't be long. I went by the clinic and picked up a syringe of morphine from the emergency box and packed it in my bag. Even with the neuropathy, the leg had to hurt. Maybe he'd take a morphine shot.

Bud's apartment light was on, and I could see figures moving behind the curtain. I knocked, and Bobby Amundsen cracked open the door and motioned me inside. A hazy curtain of smoke hung in the living room. Two empty bottles of rum were on the nightstand. Sister Mia sat on the couch nursing a glass of coffee brandy. Lisa sat with the men. They sipped their drinks quietly. Bud, his yellow-gray beard trimmed and brushed, his pale arms hanging limply on the armrests, wore his captain's hat. Once, when Bud stopped breathing, the group collectively held their breath, only to put their lips to their glasses and swallow when Bud settled into a regular rhythm once more.

"Has he been having much pain?" I asked.

"He was asking for rum, two, maybe three hours ago," Bobby answered. "It seemed to help relax him. Lately he's been doing this breathing thing, powering up regular as can be, then sputtering like he's missing a cylinder and stalling out."

I scanned Bud's face for signs of pain. His eyes were roving and unfocused.

Lisa took another sip of rum and looked down into her half-empty glass. She took a deep draw on her cigarette and leaned back on her chair. I placed my stethoscope on Bud's barrel chest and heard coarse crackles in the right lung—pneumonia, the old man's friend. It wouldn't be long now.

Bobby cleared his throat. "This is Orrin, Bud's brother. He came in on the evening ferry last night."

A short, balding man, Orrin extended a hand. He took a long look at Bud and started to speak but couldn't find the right words. "Tough old bird," Orrin finally said.

"Yeah, he's a tough old bird," Bobby agreed.

The sun was coming up as I left Bud's apartment and returned home for breakfast. Through morning hours at the health center, on the ferry ride to Portland, and on to Chebeague Island for clinic, I expected my beeper to go off with the news that Bud was gone.

At the end of the day, on my way home, I stopped at the apartment. Bud was still breathing. Lisa had dabbed his lips with Vaseline and draped a Hudson Bay wool blanket over his lap. I helped her turn Bud's recliner away from the TV, and we pulled it toward the window. The blinds were open, the curtains tied back, so that the bay was visible between Feeney's Market and the marina. I felt for a pulse. He was gone.

Amid the stack of ornate calabash and meerschaum pipes next to the recliner was a simple briar pipe. Beneath it was an unopened pouch of Sail Tobacco. I wrapped the pipe and tobacco and placed them inside a zipped compartment in my green satchel. Then I opened up my pocket calendar and wrote, *Try pipe?* As an afterthought I added, *Get better boat.*

Sister Mia registered a normal blood pressure the week after Bud Perry died. She was on three different medications to achieve this minor miracle, but I worry less about her and suspect she might outlive me. Like Bud Perry, she is a tough old bird. Knowing how Bud felt about religion, I'm not sure how he would have reacted if he'd woken one last time to see Sister Mia praying over him. Still, on some level they understood each other's world, and their friendship was a secret known to me only at the end.

Johanna is thriving back on Cliff Island. After her hip fracture, I never thought she'd leave the Seaside Nursing Home, but there she was, four months later, inviting relatives from Germany to visit her at Valhalla cottage. Twice I've taken the police boat to Cliff Island and performed a perfunctory house call. It is preordained that Johanna will take no medications, but she wanted to spend a lot of time making that decision. Despite the lack of pharmacologic assistance, she is stronger than last year and vowed to winter over, once again, on Cliff.

The week before, Hazel Towns opened her front door, walked off her porch, and crossed Sterling Street for an appointment at the health center. She chatted with two women in the waiting room who hadn't seen her in twelve years. Within an hour, the whole island knew.

When I asked her, "Why now?" She said, "I've been cooped up in that house long enough."

As the last snowdrifts melted, Ricky was making steady progress; a weekend home visit went well, a second even better. He gained back some weight. In early May he was discharged from the Augusta Mental Health Institute for good and went back to school. The bubbly innocence and enthusiasm with which he'd entered adolescence was gone, but what it was replaced with—a belief that he could go on, that he *would* go on—was enough for now. One morning on the *Machigonne*, I looked up from my newspaper and watched Ricky quietly shuffling past me to a seat in the bow. He removed his backpack and placed it on the green slatted bench. On the other side, he draped his coat. Underway, he opened a schoolbook. A classmate came aboard, picked up Ricky's backpack, and stowed it at their feet. He opened his own textbook and asked Ricky a question. The two compared notes.

Later that summer Ricky passed our house in the half-light between day and night, floating along, arms in balance, those long legs stretching out ahead, his feet touching and pushing off so lightly, he seemed to drift above the road. When I called his name, he turned his head and waved.

When I saw Ricky's mother walking down Island Avenue, past Feeney's Market, I quickened my pace and caught up with her. The burden of Ricky's illness had lifted from her, and she met me with a handshake and a smile. Hazel Towns, recognizing Mrs. Hogan from her prerecluse days, crossed the street to chat. Ricky's illness had rarely been discussed in public, but his recovery has been a quiet source of joy for the entire island. Mrs. Hogan spoke as if Hazel was familiar with every detail of Ricky's story.

When Mrs. Hogan retold the story of the visit to Tommy Reynolds's house, Hazel's expression froze; she hadn't heard anything about that night. I worried the stress of Ricky's story might trigger a relapse. For many people, even the possibility that a rape had occurred on Peaks Island would be unnerving. But for Hazel? I worried it might drive her inside again, permanently.

I harbored my own reservations about Tommy Reynolds. Certainly his banishment from the island had been a turning point for Ricky, and yet . . . I broke into the story. "Mrs. Hogan, I'm ecstatic about Ricky. I know you never gave up. He had his family behind him all the way."

"Well, don't sell yourself short, Doctor Radis. I know for a fact you had a hand in getting him better. You stuck it out with him. I know Ricky's grateful. We're all grateful."

"And yet," I paused, uncertain how to proceed. "I'm not a judge, and I'm not a jury. None of us is. Tommy must have . . . done it. Certainly he must have done it, or Ricky wouldn't have recovered. But we didn't know that then. We didn't *know* Ricky would recover." I faltered. I could see the hair stand up on the back of Mrs. Hogan's neck, and for a moment she couldn't bring herself to speak.

When she did, the words spilled from her mouth. "Let me tell you something, mister. If Bobby Amundsen hadn't gone to Tommy's house and thrown him off the island, Ricky would still be in lockdown. And that's a fact. Don't talk to me about justice. Ricky would still be waiting for justice. If Bobby hadn't held me back that night at Tommy's I would have shot the bastard." She stuck her hands in her pockets and turned as if to go.

"You know, sometimes . . ." Hazel started to say more, but held off. Her pale gray eyes scanned the bay. A monarch butterfly settled onto a clump of goldenrod next to the sidewalk and folded its wings. Then the monarch took off, zigzagging over bittersweet and goldenrod to the beach, around an abandoned rowboat, and then across the shore break, until it disappeared against the horizon. The *Machigonne*, brimming with summer tourists, idled down as she lined up to dock.

Hazel suddenly needed to find something in her canvas tote bag. She held it up to her chest and rummaged inside. Out came a can of Moxie Soda and the morning newspaper. She pushed aside a sweater and windbreaker and dug deeper. Finally she located a paperback book and, opening it, found a Casco Bay Lines ferry ticket she'd been using as a bookmark. She clasped it in her hand. A wistful smile spread across her face, smoothing the lines at the edge of her mouth.

Down the hill our neighbors streamed, pulling carts, holding briefcases, or carrying tote bags, children in tow, dogs on leashes. Among them, I silently noted, were two diabetics, four on blood pressure medication, two with arthritis, and one each with heart failure, lymphoma, and depression.

A daughter pushed her mother with Alzheimer's disease in a wheelchair. I was only too aware that the daughter's breast cancer had recently metastasized to her brain. Radiation had shrunk the tumor down to the size of a grape, but we both knew it was only a matter of time. She wouldn't be cured. Behind her, a man with a captain's hat—a younger, slimmer, more dissipated version of Bud Perry—pulled an oxygen tank, the plastic tubing curled around his ears. He stopped halfway down the hill and caught his breath. Then he went on. They all went on.

The five-minute horn blew on the *Machigonne*. Shouldering her tote and taking a deep breath, Hazel said it was time to go. Then, abruptly, like a pulled plug, her eyes dimmed. She seemed tentative and uncertain. She brought her hand up and curled a finger around her nose. Her feet seemed planted to the sidewalk. "I'm sorry," she said finally, looking down at her feet, "This isn't as easy as it looks."

Mrs. Hogan reached over and squeezed Hazel's shoulder. "Maybe another day, Hazel."

The last straggler rounded Down Front and hustled down the hill past Lisa's coffee shop. The crew loosened the dock lines and readied the gangplank for the last passenger to board. Then the captain leaned out of the pilothouse, one hand shielding his eyes from the morning sun. "Hold on, hold on. We've got another runner . . ."

Hazel's tote bag was at our feet. Down the hill she raced. As she boarded the *Machigonne*, she turned back and waved in our direction. She was on her way.

About the Author

Dr. Radis was drawn to a career in medicine after meeting a bush pilot and osteopathic family physician in Baja, Mexico. Following an internal medicine residency, the young doctor moved his family to Peaks Island off the coast of Maine and traveled by boat to the four year-round islands in Casco Bay, logging more than 100 house calls a year.

Although Dr. Radis eventually completed a fellowship in rheumatology, for more than three decades he has commuted to the mainland on his boat *DASAKAMO*. His children, Kate and Molly, attended the Peaks Island grade school—with forty students, one of the smallest grade schools in Maine—and graduated from Portland High School, where more than thirty languages are spoken by immigrant students from around the world.

Throughout his years as both a primary care physician and as a specialist, Dr. Radis has published both in peer-reviewed journals and in the popular press. He has written on the narcotic epidemic, the logic of expanding Medicare for all Americans, and medical marijuana. As the medical director for the Maine-African Partnership for Social Justice, he travels regularly to the Kiryandongo UN Settlement in Uganda, where he partners with refugee groups in innovative public health programs.

In recognition of his commitment to public health, Dr. Radis has been named both the Louis Hanson Maine Physician of the Year, and Teacher of the Year at the University of New England, College of Osteopathic Medicine—a rare achievement.